The Art & Science of Coaching Series

DEVELOPING AN OFFENSIVE GAME PLAN

Brian Billick
Minnesota Vikings

ISBN: 1-57167-046-7

Book Layout: Antonio J. Perez
Book Design: Andrea Garrett
Cover Design: Laura Griswold

Coaches Choice Books is an imprint of :   Sagamore Publishing Inc.
                                                   P.O. Box 647
                                                   Champaign, IL 61824-0647
                                                   (217) 359-5940
                                                   Fax: (217) 359-5975
                                                   Web Site: http//www.sagamorepub.com

DEDICATION

I would like to thank all the coaches with whom I have worked who have each in some way contributed to the philosophies and concepts presented in this book.

Special thanks to Erica Weiland and Steve Fedie for their help in compiling this material.

FOREWORD

The more detailed and specific a game plan can be laid out for a player, the more he can perform with confidence and efficiency. The way we install and practice our game plans with the Minnesota Vikings has been very helpful in providing me with the information and tools I need to do my job properly.

Coach Billick's detailed and comprehensive approach is one of the reasons we have been able to produce the record amount of offense we have over the last few years. The material Brian provides in this book should give you a good idea of how we prepare for a given opponent, and is designed to help you to develop a similar structure that will enable your team to perform at its highest potential.

Warren Moon
Quarterback
Minnesota Vikings

INTRODUCTION

The purpose of this book is to provide a basic overview of the steps involved in setting up and implementing an offensive game plan. Although the scope of variations facing a coach in high school, college, or professional football can be quite diverse, it is my experience that the basic fundamentals used in installing an offensive structure and game plan remain the same.

The primary focus of this book is to outline a very specific structure as to how to determine the size and scope of the offensive scheme you may be using, how to focus that package into a weekly game plan and practice format, then finally, how to lay out that plan in as direct and simple a manner as possible for both coaches and players.

My coaching experiences range from high school to small and major college to the National Football League. These experiences have shown me that in spite of the unique problems and advantages encountered at each level, the game has certain qualities that carry over from one level to the next.

You should keep in mind that even though the text includes several examples of actual plays from teams I have been associated with that have had success, they serve strictly as examples. It is not my intention to suggest a specific style of play or even a run/pass ratio.

I have had the good fortune to work with several great coaches, including Bill Walsh, Tom Landry, Dan Reeves, Denny Green, and Lavelle Edwards (Brigham Young University). Although each of these successful coaches is very different in his personality and approach to the game, there are two constants about each: 1) they are all excellent teachers; and 2) all of these individuals have a very well-defined structure to which they adhere in preparing their teams.

It is those two constants, above all else, that I have tried to maintain in my coaching career. This commitment, coupled with the viewpoints of the many talented coaches with which I have had the good fortune to work, is what I have based my philosophies on as the Offensive Coordinator of the Minnesota Vikings, and which I have outlined in this book.

Even though the situation with which you are working may vary a great deal from the problems I face in the National Football League, it is my hope that by outlining the way we approach our game plan preparation, you may be able to apply some of these principles or formulas to the preparation of your team.

For discussion purposes in this book, I will refer to your responsibility of preparing a game plan as that of the offensive coordinator. I understand that this nomenclature may not be the specific title you hold. On the other hand, whether you are performing these duties as the head coach while serving as your own play caller, or you simply have not been given the title, "offensive coordinator" best describes those responsibilities.

Define Your Job

One of the first things you should do is identify what exactly your job as the offensive coordinator is. I learned quite early in my career that the job should be taken quite literally. The title of the job is offensive "coordinator," not offensive "genius," not offensive "guru," nor offensive "mastermind."

The dictionary defines the word "coordinate" as: to arrange in proper order, harmonious adjustment, or interaction. I think the key word in this definition is "interaction."

This interaction happens on two levels. First, you must be able to interact effectively with the other members of your offensive staff. We have an excellent group of coaches with the Vikings, each with a wide variety of experiences and capabilities. It would be foolish to not utilize those capabilities by excluding them from the creation and implementation of our game plans.

Secondly, the most brilliant of game plans is useless unless it can be readily learned and executed by your players. To this end, how you install and practice your game plan is almost as, if not more, important than the selection of plays you come up with.

In an interview with Bill Walsh in the January 1993 issue of the *Harvard Business Review*, he outlined many of his philosophical approaches to the preparation of his many successful football teams. In that piece he stated, *"A system should never reduce the game to the point where it simply blames the players for failure because they did not physically overwhelm the opponent."*

Coach Walsh went on to say, *"You need to have a plan even for the worst scenario. It doesn't mean that it will always be successful. But you will always be prepared and at your best."*

At any level, you must sell your game plan every week to your players so they are confident in what is being run and are enthusiastic about the opportunities they will have by implementing your game plan. The more your players can gain a sense of confidence that they are prepared for anything that might come up, the less likely they are to feel "physically overwhelmed," even if their opponent is capable of doing just that.

As A Teacher

In arranging your game plan in "harmonious order or adjustment," it must be done in an atmosphere that maximizes the "learning curve" of your players. There is little secret that players do not perform at their best when hesitation exists in their minds about what is expected of them.

It has been proven time and again, both statistically and in practical application, that 60 minutes is *not always* enough time for the *best team* to win. It is *just enough* time for the team that *plays the best* to win.

As a coach, you will not catch a single pass, throw a single block, or score a single touchdown this season. Nor will you, on a consistent basis, make that singularly brilliant play call that wins the game.

Football is a game with very defined parameters. The very nature of the game and the geometric relationship of the field to the distances required to move the ball are very specific and definable.

The exciting part of coaching for me is knowing I can affect the game by providing as much information as possible to my team in preparing them for what they will face during the course of a game.

In his book *The Road Ahead,* Microsoft founder Bill Gates defines "information" as the *"reduction of uncertainty."* The information you provide your offensive personnel must reduce their uncertainty as much as possible, if you expect them to execute your game plan with confidence and without hesitation or uncertainty.

This is not to say you can "program" any specific player to be better than he is. I often tell my players that there are two types of players I *cannot* have: One is a player who *cannot do* what he is told, the other is a player who *can only do* exactly what he is told. At some point the players' God-given talents, character, and drive to succeed must take control. However, you as a coach have a responsibility to provide those players with information and a structure that will allow their abilities to flourish.

I have no delusions about the offensive success we have had with the Vikings the last few years. With players like Warren Moon, Chris Carter, Jake Reed, Amp Lee, and Randall McDaniel, it is clearly the talents and character of these types of players that have been the cornerstone of the record-breaking production. I can, however, take a great deal of satisfaction in knowing that we coaches have, at the very least, provided a platform for those great athletes to accomplish what they have.

One of the secrets to providing this information is to consolidate the amount of information they have to process into a workable, learnable level. It is quite evident that players today are products of the "video generation." Materials presented to them must "grab" their attention in the manner in which they are accustomed. Simply standing up at a chalkboard and bludgeoning them with your game plan is not optimizing the "learning curve" your players are used to.

As a coach/teacher, it is your responsibility to continually search for new and innovative ways to provide your players with the information they need. If the game has changed in the last few years, it has been less in terms of the fundamental approach to the X's and O's than in the technological ways they are prepared.

Many coaches, particularly young coaches coming into the profession, are finding a number of creative and helpful ways to use personal computers in the analysis and preparation of football-related materials.

Although many coaches are still uncomfortable with this new technology and therefore dismiss it as being too fancy for their needs, the use of computers can enhance your production just like it has in any number of other professions. It is a way to analyze and present a large amount of information in a more concise and organized manner.

I believe the computer is one of the best "teaching" tools available to you. Much like the use of video compared to film, the advances in available technology can make a big difference in presenting your materials to your players. Accordingly, this book includes several examples of how the Vikings staff uses computers to analyze and present our materials to our team. Most of these methods are available to you with the simplest of computer programs in the form of spreadsheets (Excel, Lotus...), word processing (Word Perfect, Microsoft Word...), or drawing programs (Super Paint, Visio...). How these teaching aids can be used by coaches is looked at in more detail later in this book.

Elements of Preparation

The process of developing an offensive game plan will be examined in four main areas:

- Determine size and scope of the offense
- Outline situational offensive needs
- Implementations of game plan
- Game day needs

First, we will look at the overall approach of how much offense is needed in any given year, week, or game. Determining the size of your offensive package is the most fundamental of questions that must be answered before you can begin to formulate an offensive game plan.

Once we have established these parameters, we will look at the actual elements that make up each segment of "situational offense" that you must account for in a game plan. This step will be broken down in the following manner:

- Base Offense
- 3rd Down
- Pre-Red Zone
- Red Zone
- Special Categories

Each situational area will be discussed and outlined as to size, scope, and special considerations given to each.

Next, we will examine how the game plan is formulated and presented to the team, and what allocation of time should be given to each situational area in meetings and practice. Finally, game plan layout will address the way in which the final game plan is laid out and implemented on game day.

How Does This Apply To You

In each of these sections, the materials will be discussed with regards to the way the Minnesota Vikings approach each situation with *our* desired ratio of run to pass, drop back to play action, zone protection vs. man protection, inside running game vs. outside running game, etc.

These examples are just that: examples. It is not the intent of this book to advocate a particular style of play, but to outline a structured approach to implement whatever your particular philosophies may be.

The phrase "West Coast Offense" is probably one of the most popular and yet misused phrases in the coaching lexicon today. Many people think of it as a specific style of runs or passes that emulates the success of the San Francisco 49ers during the 1980s and now into the '90s. Although this style of play can be traced as far back as Sid Gilman and Paul Brown of the early AFL days, it was clearly Bill Walsh who consolidated and refined the basic concepts of this philosophy.

However, when I think of Bill Walsh and the "West Coast Offense," I think less of the actual X's and O's than I do of the comprehensive approach Coach Walsh took to creating a structure. That structure was based on specific teaching methods that carried a team systematically from installation in training camp, to weekly installation of the game plans and practices, to the actual implementation on game day.

It is this systematic approach, which I learned from people like Bill Walsh and Dennis Green, that I am attempting to convey in this book. Regardless of the style of play your advocate, the overall structure of preparing your team through the game plan remains the same.

Measurable Probabilities

As we examine the important parameters of situational offense, it will be helpful to keep in mind a couple of focal points that have a direct effect on the outcome of a game.

A number of studies focused on probability and statistical measures have been conducted over the last two decades in the NFL in hopes of developing a valid shortlist of priorities in which the team winning a game was significantly more productive than the team that lost that particular game.

Although research suggests that any number of variables can and will intervene to affect performance and the outcome of a game, over the last few years a clear-cut pattern has been established. From year to year, four factors have been identified that have a consistently high correlation to a team's winning or losing:

- Turnovers
- Explosive plays
- 1st down efficiency
- Red Zone efficiency

Turnovers have long been recognized as a major determinant of the outcome of a game. A team with a positive turnover ratio in any given game has between a 75-85% better chance of winning a game than its opponent. This is an interactive measurable because it has to do with the giveaway-takeaway relationship of both offense and defense. The advantage of a team who has a high takeaway margin is negated if their offense is giving up the ball at the same ratio, and vice versa.

Explosive plays are measured by the NFL as gains of 20 yards or more. A more detailed analysis shows a more valid measure being runs of 12 yards or more and passes of 16 yards or more. These levels of production proved to be more significant as to what is needed to constitute and gain the effects of an "explosion". The 1994 and '95 NFL seasons were the first in a dozen years that explosions carried a higher winning ratio than did turnovers. This measurement showed that a team with a +2 or greater advantage won the game between 80-85% of the time. The significant thing about explosives is that they do not necessarily need to lead to a score to be productive. Huge changes of field position can also positively change the profile of a game. This measurement, like turnovers, is an interactive measurable because a team's effectiveness in this area can be diminished if your defense is giving up explosives at the same rate as the offense is gaining them.

1st down (+4 yds.) efficiency has a direct effect on your ability to stay on schedule with your play calling by maintaining a 3rd and medium-to-short ratio as much as possible. The two keys to this measurable are running effectively on first down (about 45%) and completing a high percentage of passes (better than 60%).

The range or efficiency in this situation will run between 40-50%. Although this does not appear to be a huge difference from the worst teams to the best, it is significant when you consider that your 1st down calls constitute between 40-45% of your total plays run in a year. These percentages may seem low to you with regards to being highly effective but a closer look at the top 1st down efficiency teams in the NFL in 1995 will show you how consistent these levels are:

TEAM	1ST DOWNS	+4 PLAYS	%
VIKINGS	490	238	49%
BEARS	467	232	50%
DOLPHINS	472	232	50%
49ERS	480	232	49%

Red Zone efficiency (percentage of scores vs. number of series) becomes an important measurable because you are talking about scores. The key note to make here is the importance of scoring any points — touchdowns or field goals — as being efficient. This will be discussed in much more detail in the chapter dealing with the Red Zone.

A perfect example of how these measurable categories have a direct effect on the ability of a team to win was in the Vikings' 1993 season. That season was a transition year for us with the loss of three of our starting five offensive linemen from the Central Division Championship team of 1992. In addition, we had a new quarterback in Jim McMahon. We also lost Terry Allen, a 1,000 yard rusher the previous season, during the pre-season.

In spite of this, we were able to win four of our last five games (against four playoff teams and three division winners) to earn a spot in the playoffs. We were able to accomplish this by being among the top teams in the League in three of the four measurable categories: 1st down efficiency, turnovers, and Red Zone efficiency.

In 1993, the Vikings ranked fourth in the NFL in 1st down +4 efficiency, fourth in the League in fewest turnovers, and first in the NFL in Red Zone efficiency at 96%.

Although you will have to be concerned with many variables in establishing your play calling, we have found that these four measurable categories are significant enough to warrant considerable attention. We will refer to these measurable categories periodically when talking about priorities for each offensive situation.

Summary
The key elements in designing and developing your offensive package are:

1)   *Define your job* as "offensive coordinator" and the approach you will take.

2)   Recognize that above all else you are a teacher and *determine the capabilities* of your students/players and the best *methods of teaching/coaching* them.

3)   Focus on four main elements when preparing any game plan:
    • Determining size and scope of the offense
    • Outlining situational offensive needs
    • Implementation of game plan
    • Game day needs

4) Remember that the number one factor in approaching each of the aforementioned four elements is to be as *detailed and specific* as your time and materials allow.

5) Keep the *four "key" measurable categories* in mind when formulating your game plan:
   - Turnovers
   - Explosive plays
   - 1st down efficiency
   - Red Zone efficiency

CONTENTS

                                                                        Page

Dedication 3

Foreword 4

Introduction 5

Chapter

1   How Much Offense 15

2   Base Offense 27

3   3rd Down 43

4   Pre-Red Zone 55

5   Red Zone 57

6   Special Categories 63

7   Installing the Offense 71

8   Game Day 83

9   The Soap Box 87

10   Summary Points 95

About the Author 101

How Much Offense?

Two of the most fundamental questions you need to ask are:

- How much offense can I run during a season?
- How much offense can be effectively practiced and run each week?

Keep in mind that the amount of offense you can handle may be vastly different than what your players can handle. As any teacher knows, you must teach/coach to your least common denominator.

Part of your job as offensive coordinator is to make sure you are using the plays and techniques that best fit the abilities of your players. This may change from year to year based on the turnover of your personnel. We in the NFL are now dealing with the same problems of player turnover that those of you coaching high school and college have been facing your entire careers.

With the advent of free agency in the NFL, most teams are experiencing a 20-25% yearly turnover. Hence, like in high school and college, you could have a total roster turnover every four years.

Although certain key players (like a quarterback) may be tied up contractually for longer periods of time, the turnover of the rest of the offense is something one has to consider every year when determining how much offense the team can carry over from one year to the next.

In determining the amount of offense with which you can deal, you must think on three levels:

- Yearly
- Weekly
- Game Day

Each level has very set parameters as to how much offense will actually be run in any given segment. The more you can overlap the amount of total offense you can carry vs. the amount that can be effectively practiced, the more effective the offense you actually run on game day will be.

It is impossible to accurately predict the exact amount of offense you will use in any given game. There is always going to be a certain amount of overage that has to be built in for the "what if's". For example, "what if" they blitz more than you had thought?; "what if" you aren't able to run the ball as well as you thought?; "what if" your quarterback is having an off day?; or "what if" the weather is bad?

We have tried to keep our overage to between 25-30 percent of the total game snaps we can predict. This percent of overage is something we will work very hard to maintain. Each week I examine how much of the offensive game plan was actually used vs. what was installed and practiced, looking to see if it can be pared down.

You have to be careful about not limiting yourself too much, though. Many assistant coaches may try to eliminate too much offense because it makes less for them to have to prepare. You don't want to waste time working on things you are never going to use, but you must have all that you need to get the job done.

Graphically, what we are talking about looks like this:

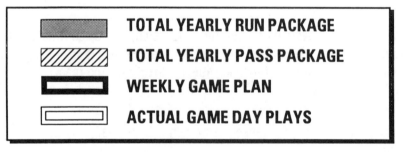

�	**TOTAL YEARLY RUN PACKAGE**
	TOTAL YEARLY PASS PACKAGE
	WEEKLY GAME PLAN
	ACTUAL GAME DAY PLAYS

Diagram 1-1 represents a basic offensive package balanced between runs and passes. In this example, the game plan and actual game day calls fell within the expected norms you set going into the game. This is obviously a winning profile where the amount of offense practiced and used matched each other very well.

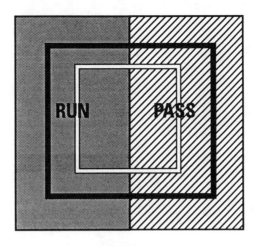

DIAGRAM 1-1

Diagrams 1-2 and 1-3 represent the same offense but with a different game plan. In this example the game plan calls for the passing game to be a little more prominent, possibly because your opponent plays really good run defense, or perhaps because their secondary is highly vulnerable.

Diagram 1-2 shows that the game went according to your plan and you were able to throw the ball effectively.

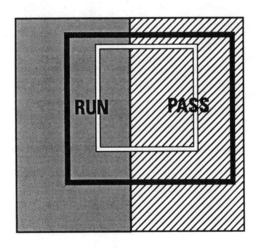

DIAGRAM 1-2

Diagram 1-3 is an example of the same approach but once you actually played the game you found you were able to run the ball more effectively than you thought and pushed that aspect of the game plan more. Again, both examples showed you planned well and were very efficient in your preparation and were able to stay with your basic game plan.

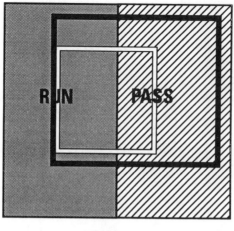

DIAGRAM 1-3

Diagrams 1-4 and 1-5 are examples of the same game plans by a team whose base game plan this week is focused more on the run.

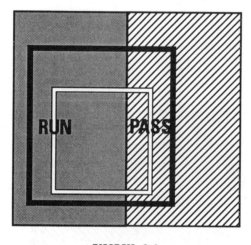

DIAGRAM 1-4

In Diagram 1-4, the game plan went according to schedule with the run being the main focus.

In Diagram 1-5, that same game plan obviously could not establish the run the way it was designed. Not only did this team have to rely more on the pass, but it was forced to draw on part of its base passing attack that was not practiced during the week.

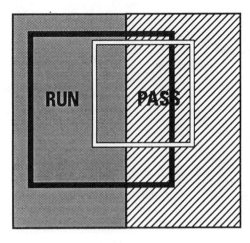

DIAGRAM 1-5

Ideally, you would like to keep this type of play calling to a minimum. Often, however, there may be a base part of your attack that you have used enough during the year that even though you may not have emphasized it during the week, you are still comfortable coming back to it in any given game.

Diagrams 1-6 and 1-7 show the approach of a team whose primary yearly offensive structure is based more on the run.

In Diagram 1-6 the game plan obviously went according to plan.

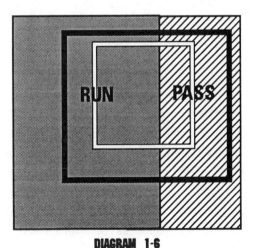

DIAGRAM 1-6

Diagram 1-7 is an example of a game we would all like to avoid. This example shows that the base game day calls were not effective and you had to go to other aspects

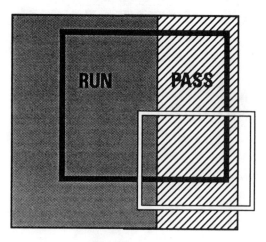

DIAGRAM 1-7

of the offense that were not emphasized during the week. Furthermore, you apparently got desperate enough you had to make things up as you went along, outside of your basic offensive structure.

Obviously if you find yourself in this situation too often, you must go back and re-examine whether you are using the best offense available for your personnel, and also re-examine the way you are selecting and practicing your game plans.

Keep these examples in mind as we look at the size and scope of the offense we discuss, both as a whole and in certain situations. I think it will become quite clear to you what we are talking about when we discuss the parameters of how much your offensive package, weekly game plans and game day calls encompass.

Numbers of Plays

To help determine the size of your offensive package (yearly, weekly and game day), some parameters need to be set with regard to the actual number of plays run in a game. Again, keep in mind that the examples provided in this book are based on the last four years of the Minnesota Vikings and the NFL. A chart illustrating the offensive circumstances of seven different NFL teams for the 1995 season gives an overview of the variances between teams and specific situations:

This cross section of examples uses teams from different conferences and divisions, different styles of play and different success rates. In spite of the differences, it is easy to see how consistent the play ratios remain.

OVERALL	MINN	DENVER	CHICAGO	GREEN BAY	PITTS	SAN DIEGO	WASH	AVG	PER
1ST DOWN	465	441	480	482	480	440	454	463	28.9
2ND LONG	224	214	195	228	229	238	233	223	13.9
2ND MED	122	111	132	111	120	87	100	112	7.0
2ND 1	24	33	20	20	19	26	13	22	1.4
3RD 11+	42	32	17	28	35	35	39	33	2.0
3RD 7-10	70	86	74	80	71	80	99	80	5.0
3RD 4-6	62	48	61	51	65	64	57	58	3.6
3RD 2-3	34	30	30	49	32	32	36	35	2.2
3RD 1	33	28	33	26	26	15	14	25	1.6
4TH	10	19	22	6	26	19	17	17	1.1
	1,086	1,042	1,064	1,081	1,103	1,036	1,062	1,068	66.7

All of these teams ran slightly more plays than the NFL average. The average number of total plays run in a year in the NFL the last two seasons was 986 (1994) and 997 (1995), or about 62 plays a game. Compare these numbers with the Vikings' overall numbers the last four years, detailed in the chart below.

Again, you can see how similar the ratios are, even though there was a great difference between the production and style of our 1992-93 season and the 1994-95 seasons.

OVERALL	1992	1993	1994	1995	AVG	PER
1ST DOWN	420	417	458	465	440	27.50
2ND LONG	216	206	241	224	222	13.88
2ND MED	95	115	113	122	111	6.94
2ND 1	27	19	15	24	21	1.31
3RD 11+	27	36	30	42	34	2.13
3RD 7-10	56	66	94	70	72	4.50
3RD 4-6	50	50	40	62	51	3.19
3RD 2-3	42	36	46	34	40	2.50
3RD 1	34	25	25	33	29	1.81
4TH	9	5	14	10	10	0.63
	976	975	1,076	1,086	1,030	64

In the last four years, the Minnesota Vikings ran 1076 (1994) and 1081 (1995) plays for the third and sixth highest totals during that period. This averages out to about 68 and 67 plays a game, respectively. During that same period, Tampa Bay ran 905 (1995) plays for the lowest number of plays, averaging 56 plays a game.

In 1992 and 1993, the Vikings were a much more run-oriented team and finished 13th and 11th in the NFL in total offense. During the period we started three different quarterbacks and six different running backs. As we discussed earlier, our Base Offense (run/pass ratio) was dramatically different for these two years than the next two.

In that last two years when we finished 3rd and 4th in total offense in the NFL, respectively, the averages were obviously pushed up.

These numbers need to be broken down further if we are to examine the size and scope of our game plan discussions:

OPEN FIELD:	1992	1993	1994	1995	AVG	PER	
1ST SERIES	162	159	167	163	163	10.17	
1ST 10+	5	12	15	19	13	0.80	
1ST EARNED	156	161	177	179	168	10.52	
1ST 9-	1	0	1	2	1	0.06	
2ND LONG	175	162	189	174	175	10.94	
2ND MED	69	88	84	77	80	4.97	
2ND 1	14	11	9	17	13	0.80	
3RD 11+	20	33	26	30	27	1.70	
3RD 7-10	46	48	66	55	54	3.36	
3RD 4-6	39	33	35	46	38	2.39	
3RD 2-3	29	26	30	20	26	1.64	
3RD 1	24	16	17	22	20	1.23	
4TH	5	4	5	3	4	0.27	49
RED ZONE:							
1ST SERIES	9	7	4	12	8	0.50	
1ST 10+	2	1	4	3	3	0.16	
1ST EARNED	60	51	70	63	61	3.81	
1ST GOAL	25	26	20	24	24	1.48	
2ND LONG	41	44	52	50	47	2.92	
2ND MED	26	27	29	45	32	1.98	
2ND 1	13	8	6	7	9	0.53	
3RD 11+	7	3	4	12	7	0.41	
3RD 7-10	10	18	28	15	18	1.11	
3RD 4-6	11	17	5	16	12	0.77	
3RD 2-3	13	10	16	14	13	0.83	
3RD 1	10	9	7	11	10	0.59	
4TH	4	1	9	7	5	0.33	15
	976	975	1,076	1,086	1,028	64	

The values in these situational breakdowns are what we will use in our discussion in each area about the amount of offense needed. The averages in each area will help us set the parameters for the size of the offensive package we need and ultimately the amount of offense we will use each week.

These numbers stay amazingly consistent from year to year and even from team to team. We will use the same seven teams from the earlier overall example to illustrate this.

OPEN FIELD:	MINN	DENVER	CHICAGO	GREEN BAY	PITTS	SAN DIEGO	WASH	AVG	PER
1ST DOWN	363	350	356	378	370	354	355	361	22.6
2ND LONG	174	177	152	184	178	195	185	178	11.1
2ND MED	77	76	84	80	80	64	70	76	4.7
2ND 1	17	23	13	14	9	19	7	15	0.9
3RD 11+	30	29	16	27	26	23	32	26	1.6
3RD 7-10	55	70	55	63	47	64	80	62	3.9
3RD 4-6	46	31	37	38	47	56	39	42	2.6
3RD 2-3	20	21	24	30	24	17	19	22	1.4
3RD 1	22	17	23	19	21	11	9	17	1.1
4TH	3	13	13	3	10	13	7	9	0.6
									50.6

RED ZONE	MINN	DENVER	CHICAGO	GREEN BAY	PITTS	SAN DIEGO	WASH	AVG	PER
1ST DOWN	78	63	79	74	75	63	74	72	4.5
2ND LONG	50	37	43	44	51	43	48	45	2.8
2ND MED	45	35	48	31	40	23	30	36	2.3
2ND 1	7	10	7	6	10	7	6	8	0.5
3RD 11+	13	3	1	1	9	12	7	6	0.4
3RD 7-10	15	16	19	17	24	16	19	18	1.1
3RD 4-6	16	17	24	13	18	8	18	16	1.0
3RD 2-3	14	9	6	19	8	15	17	13	0.8
3RD 1	11	11	10	7	5	4	5	8	0.5
4TH	7	6	9	3	16	6	10	8	0.5
1ST GOAL	24	28	45	30	35	23	25	30	1.9
									16.3

Your actual numbers will vary by the level of play, number of games played in a year, and to a small degree, the type of offense you run. The differences usually are no more than 10-15%.

A breakdown of the same ratios by the 1989-91 Stanford University teams shows similar results:

OPEN FIELD:	1989	1990	1991	AVG	PER
			STANFORD		
1ST DOWN	138	142	135	138	13
1ST EARNED	152	152	148	151	14
2ND LONG	149	133	136	139	13
2ND MED	68	69	62	66	6
2ND 1	12	12	11	12	1
3RD 7+	65	63	52	60	5
3RD 4-6	34	52	52	46	4
3RD 2-3	24	26	21	24	2
3RD 1	12	11	10	11	1
4TH	4	10	3	6	1

Most college teams, however, traditionally run more plays during a game. For example, in 1995, the average major college team ran 795 plays, over 11 games, for about 72 plays a game.

As is usually the case with statistics, they can be very accurate, yet completely wrong at the same time. The average American family consists of 2.3 children. This statistic is completely accurate. However, how many families do you know that have exactly 2.3 children? Get my point?

These numbers can be very helpful in determining ratios and parameters, but you must keep in mind that every team and game is different and there are going to be "anticipated" fluctuations from game to game.

In subsequent chapters in this book, these numbers and ratios are referred to a good deal in outlining the amount of offense you need to account for in each offensive situational category.

Summary

The key elements in determining how much offense you should carry are:

1) Think on *three levels* in determining how much offense you can run: *yearly, weekly and on game day.*
2) Take the time to *determine exactly* the *size and scope* of each critical situation you will face.
3) Work hard to *keep your overage* of plays to *25-30%.*
4) Take the time to *review each week* the amount and nature of offense you ran and see if your planning stayed within the *expected norms* you set for yourself.

CHAPTER 2

Base Offense

We quite naturally begin our game plan with our open field base offense. This will be done with particular attention given to our "Openers."

As we do with all the situational sections, let's first examine the amount of offense we will need in this section.

Based on your open field segment of your game plan, 1st down requires about 45% of your total calls in the Open Field. 2nd down requires about 35%, and 3rd and 4th downs take up the remaining 20%.

Our base package will encompass all 1st and 2nd downs:

OPEN FIELD:	1992	1993	1994	1995	AVG	PER
1ST SERIES	162	159	167	163	163	10
1ST 10+	5	12	15	19	13	1
1ST EARNED	156	161	177	179	168	11
1ST 9-	1	0	1	2	1	1
2ND LONG	175	162	189	174	175	11
2ND MED	69	88	84	77	80	5
2ND 1	14	11	9	17	13	1

As you can see, our 1st down package will consist of about 23-25 calls per game; 2nd and Long (7+ yds.) constitutes about 11-12 calls per game, while 2nd and medium (2-6 yds.) has only about 5-6 per game. 2nd and 1 in the Open Field usually comes up only once a game.

It is quite evident that your 1st downs to open a series and earned 1st downs take up most of the 1st down calls. 1st and 10+ or 1st and less than 10 (usually 1st and 5 after a penalty) are speciality calls we will discuss later.

Equally as evident is that the number of 2nd and long calls usually double that of 2nd and medium.

One of the first analyses you will want to do is to determine if a team significantly separates its defensive scheme from 1st down and 2nd and long.

Many teams will just continue their base calls from 1st down into 2nd and long, while others will change their coverage package to accommodate the long down and distance. Still other defensive teams may actually blitz more in this situation anticipating more passing on your part.

Certainly if a team just continues its normal defensive posture in 2nd and long, it allows more carryover and more continuity if you can simply extend your 1st down package into the 10-12 plays of 2nd and long.

It is my experience that most teams have a separate package for their 2nd and medium calls. This is a more advantageous down and distance for the offense in that you have a much better chance to remain balanced with run, pass, and play actions and still get a 1st down.

Although a good deal more pressure exists in making your 3rd down calls, I find 3rd down offense one of the simpler areas to prepare for. Like any other situation, the number of plays you will need are very defined and most defenses have very specific and identifiable packages on 3rd down.

The average team in the NFL faces about 200-220 3rd down situations a year. That averages out to about 12-14 calls a game. On the average, 10 of those will fall in the Open Field while 2-4 will be needed in the Red Zone.

The 3rd down ratios look like this:

OPEN FIELD:	1992	1993	1994	1995	AVG	PER
3RD 11+	20	33	26	30	27	2
3RD 7-10	46	48	66	55	54	3
3RD 4-6	39	33	35	46	38	2
3RD 2-3	29	26	30	20	26	2
3RD 1	24	16	17	22	20	1

I discuss the purpose and approach we take by breaking 3rd down up in this manner later in the 3rd down chapter. For more basic purposes, I simply break 3rd down into three areas by yardage : Long (7+), Medium (2-6) and Short (1).

The last two years the Vikings have faced 241 and 239 3rd down situations, respectively. This is a good news/bad news scenario. The good news is you are generating a great deal of offense; the bad news is that by producing this many plays, you have forced yourself into more critical 3rd down calls.

A direct correlation exists between the number of total plays run and the number of 3rd down plays. This is one of the most consistent variables in the NFL, with virtually every team falling between the norms. Regardless of whether it is a good team or a bad, passing team or running team, all teams face a 3rd down conversion every 4th or 5th play of a series.

NFL	AVG TOTAL PLAYS	AVG #3RD DOWNS	PER
1995	997	218	4.57
1994	989	219	4.52
1993	968	215	4.50
1992	918	204	4.50

Having worked through this long maze of numbers, we can now put them together to identify exactly what our starting point is and how we can build our game plan from there.

NUMBER OF PLAYS NEEDED

What we have seen to this point is that very specific and unidentifiable parameters exist within which we can isolate how much offense is required in each situational offense category.

The following table shows the numbers broken down and the situations we have discussed so far:

GAME PLAN RATIO CHART FOR OPEN FIELD							
	1ST DOWN	2ND LONG	2ND MED	2ND SHORT	3RD LONG	3RD MED	3RD SHORT
TOTAL PLAYS	20	10	5	1	5	5	1
1ST HALF PLAYS	10	5	3	1	3	3	1
RUNS	5	2	2	1		1	1
DROP BACK	2	2			3	1	
QUICKS	1	1				1	
PLAY ACTION	2		1	1			1

It is very easy to see how we have worked ourselves into isolating the specific plays with which we want to begin our game plan.

Take 1st down as the initial example. We start with the recognition that we will be making about 20 1st down calls in the open field. We then cut that in half to start with the 10 opening 1st half open field calls.

This example is of a team who strives to have a balanced run/pass ratio on 1st down. With this in mind, you should break your 1st down openers into five runs and five passes.

In a 2nd and long situation, we would like to maintain at least a 70/30 pass/run ratio and would prefer a 60/40 split. With this in mind, we script five plays for the first half with three passes and two runs.

A 2nd and medium situation constitutes about five plays a game, so we script three for the first half with a 2/1 run/pass ratio.

Furthermore, we have isolated that we want our opening passes to be 2 dropbacks, 1 quick, and 2 play actions. As we carry this thinking out over all the open field situations, you end up with your total opening play ratio:

RUNS:	12
PASSES:	16
DROP BACK:	8
QUICKS:	3
PLAY ACTION:	5

As an example of our opening 12 runs, two of them will be in short yardage situations and may in fact be the same play. Likewise, the run we have scheduled for 3rd and long may be the same run we intend for 3rd and medium. That being the case, that leaves you with 10 opening runs.

Those 10 runs do not have to be 10 different plays. They more likely would be three or four different runs from two or three different formations.

It would stand to reason that we would want to build the five play action passes off those runs and formations.

Of the three quicks we choose to throw, we may want to link them to two of the formations from which we are throwing our eight dropback passes, or one or two of the run formations, and so on.

How much carryover you wish to have from your 1st and 2nd down plays to your 3rd down calls is certainly up to you. You may want to draw from your base throws and simply change the formations, or you may want to give them a complete new set of plays.

Once you have established the priority of your opening plays, you can expand on that package to the point of even doubling those initial 30 plays to have a base Open Field package of 60 plays, with your average 50 open field calls coming from that package. This certainly fits within the limits we set earlier of about 20% overage in your preparation.

I want to reemphasize that these ratios are examples of a specific offensive philosophy, and while the approach can remain the same, the run/pass ratio can be whatever fits your offensive package.

The following diagram illustrates a profile of the team we saw earlier in the Introduction section of this book that bases its offensive package on a more run-oriented emphasis:

This team's opening sequence ratio may look more like the following:

	1ST DOWN	2ND LONG	2ND MED	2ND SHORT	3RD LONG	3RD MED	3RD SHORT
TOTAL PLAYS	20	10	5	1	5	5	1
1ST HALF PLAYS	10	5	3	1	3	3	1
RUNS	7	3	2	1	1	1	1
DROP BACK		1			3		
QUICKS	1	1				1	
PLAY ACTION	2		1	1		1	1

RUNS:	16
PASSES:	12
DROPBACK:	4
QUICKS:	3
PLAY ACTION:	6

This team clearly has established its intention to run the ball more and subsequently throw more play action passes than drop back passes.

This same approach can be applied in the Red Zone where the remaining 25% (18 plays) of your offense will be called.

These ratios and the approach we take in each situational area will be discussed in the chapters talking about those specific areas of emphasis.

By breaking your play selection down to this specific focus, it allows you to be very detailed about what it is you want to run and how each play can work in relationship to each other. This approach is the basis for establishing your "openers".

Openers
Considerable interest has been focused on the concept of "openers," whether it be the famous "25 Openers" Bill Walsh utilized, to the programmed shifting and motioning of Joe Gibbs' Redskins teams.

What this concept boils down to is a very specific and detailed approach to your opening game plan. As far back as 1979 at the American Football Coach Association National Convention, Bill Walsh — in his clinic talk called "Controlling the Ball with the Passing Game" — labeled the establishing of your openers as "the single most valuable thing that you can do as far as the game plan is concerned."

At a minimum, establishing your openers should accomplish the following things:

- *Allows you to make decisions in the cool and calm of your office during the week after a thorough analysis of your opponent.*

This philosophy is the basis from which the entire offense and game plan structure begins. It recognizes that even the best of game day coaches must plan ahead for all contingencies if the problems that a team will inevitably face each week are going to be handled effectively.

In the *Harvard Business Review* article with Bill Walsh that was cited earlier, Walsh stated, "Making judgments under severe stress is the most difficult thing there is. The more preparation you have prior to the conflict, the more you can do in a clinical situation, the better off you will be. I want to make certain that we have accounted for every critical situation."

- *Allows you to determine a desirable pass/run ratio.*

We work very hard at maintaining an equal balance on 1st down between run and pass. This is one of the few downs on which the defense has to guess a little regarding what your run/pass ratio may be. In 1995, our Open Field 1st down pass/run ratio by our main personnel groupings looked like this:

Personnel	Pass	Run
2 backs/1 TE/ 2 WO	70	67
1 back/ 2 TE/2 WO	54	53
2 backs/3 WO	14	14

The only way to consistently maintain this type of 50/50 balance is through effectively scripting such balance through your openers.

There is nothing wrong with having tendencies. Anything you do well is going to have a certain level of predictability. Too many coaches talk themselves out of running certain things just because they know the defense knows what is coming.

Make your opponent prove they can stop a strength before you change what you do just to go against your tendencies.

A world of difference exists between being predictable because you are unaware of a tendency and doing what you do best and making a defense show you they can stop you.

- *Allows you to make full usage of formations and personnel by making the run and pass interactive.*

By controlling the sequencing of your openers, you can be much more detailed in creating legitimate play action and action passes from formation and personnel groupings that will be used early in the game plan.

This also gives those players who have a limited role in the offense, (but have a certain number of plays they are being counted on to help run), a chance to see exactly what and where they have a chance to contribute.

- *Gives you a chance to challenge the defense and see what adjustments the defense may have based on your different formations and personnel.*

Openers are an excellent way to test the defense to see what the defense's game plan is, based on your formations and personnel. By anticipating what those adjustments might be, you can then expand on those things you think will be successful based on the defense's adjustments.

If you have an idea of how the defense is going to adjust to a certain motion and have a play that has "explosive" potential, you may script a more basic play in your openers from that same motion to re-confirm that the defense is indeed going to react the way you anticipated.

- *Gives your assistant coaches a specific focus as to what is being run and what they should watch for.*

This is one of the most important reasons for establishing your openers and making sure the rest of your staff is aware of what and when plays will be called. By knowing ahead of time what to expect and when, your staff can be much more effective in watching for key elements of a defense leading up to a call.

For example, if you have planned a number of draws in the opening sequence based on the upfield rush of the defense and you have informed your assistants of your plans, they can more effectively watch your opponent and see if indeed the defense is "getting up the field" to the degree you anticipated.

There is nothing more frustrating than a coach "after the fact" saying, "I didn't think that was going to work because of the way they were rushing." If they have an idea that the draw is coming they can suggest alternative plays if the defense is not giving you what you want.

- *Gives the players, especially the QB, an excellent chance to get into a rhythm, being able to anticipate the next call.*

When an offense is in "rhythm", a certain offensive pacing exists in the huddle as well as at the line of scrimmage. When players have practiced a certain sequence of plays, they tend to derive a great deal of confidence from having experienced this sequencing before. Ultimately, that confidence will show up in their execution of the game plan.

If you can maintain a rhythm, it also puts a great deal of pressure on a defensive co-ordinator to come up with something that will stop your momentum. This may put him in a situation where he makes a desperate call and puts his team in a position to give up an "explosive" play.

- *Allows you to script specific "special" plays and increases your chances of actually getting them run.*

Most teams will have a couple of "special" plays as part of their game plan. This could be a new route combination or some type of reverse. Often times these plays get practiced but are not called in the game because they are not a basic part of your mental calling sequence. By scripting them in as a part of your openers, you have a much greater chance of getting them run, and can control the specific situation in which you are looking to run them.

- *If your "Openers" are successful, it will give your offense a tremendous amount of confidence.*

Naturally, when an offense scores, a certain level of confidence is generated. That confidence is multiplied ten-fold when that scoring sequence has been laid out ahead of time in the classroom and on the practice field. In 1995, for example, the Vikings scored on 50% of our opening drives.

- *Allows you a great deal of versatility and enables your offense to look very multifaceted and diverse to a defense without having to run a large or unruly number of different plays.*

It is obviously an advantage to the offense if you can take some of the aggressiveness out of the defense. By scripting the proper sequence of openers, the offense can confuse and cause hesitation in the defense as it tries to adjust to a number of different looks and plays. If done properly, the offense can create this hesitation without using a huge or unmanageable number of plays.

Let's take the example of the opening ratios we set earlier in this chapter and build an opening sequence.

	1ST DOWN	2ND LONG	2ND MED	2ND SHORT
TOTAL PLAYS	20	10	5	1
1ST HALF PLAYS	10	5	3	1
RUNS	5	2	2	1
PASSES	5	3	1	1
DROP BACK	2	2		
QUICKS	1	1		
PLAY ACTION	2		1	1

With this play ratio, let's start with two main formations: Regular and two tights.

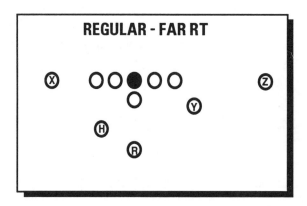

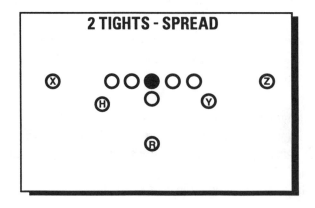

The following pages offer examples of play sequencing off these two basic formations based on the aforementioned hypothetical opening play ratio: 4 dropbacks, 2
quicks and 4 play action passes.

	TIGER(SPREAD)	**REGULAR (FAR-STR MOTION)**
RUNS	INSIDE ZONE	WEAKSIDE ISO
	TRAP	INSIDE ZONE
	OUTSIDE ZONE	STRONG SIDE ZONE (STR MOTION)
		DRAW
		TRAP
		WEAKSIDE PITCH

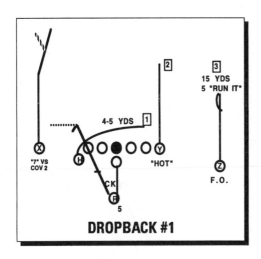

DROPBACK #1

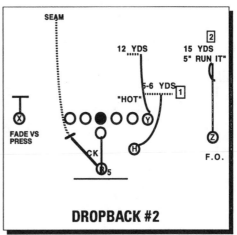

DROPBACK #2

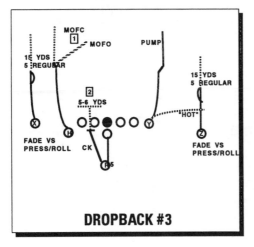

DROPBACK #3

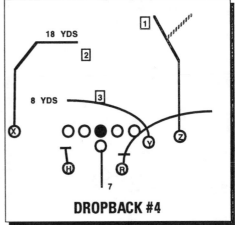

DROPBACK #4

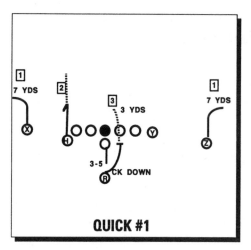

QUICK #1

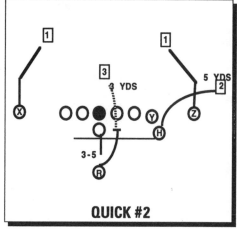

QUICK #2

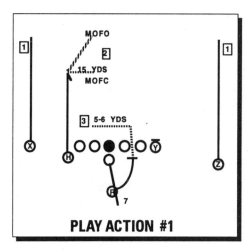

PLAY ACTION #1

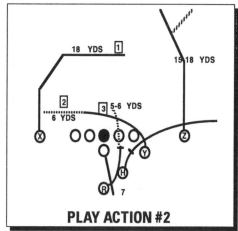

PLAY ACTION #2

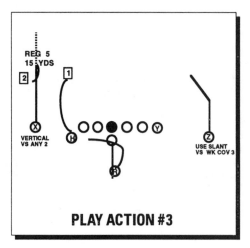

PLAY ACTION #3

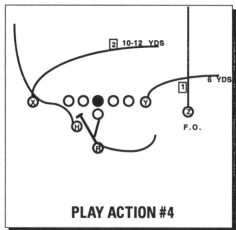

PLAY ACTION #4

Set Priorities

Your opening sequences on 1st and 2nd down should maintain three main objectives:

- Get a 1st down
- Keep yourself in a convertible 3rd down distance
- Create an "Explosive"

Much of the attention of generating 1st downs is focused on your 3rd down package. However, only 25-35% of a team's 1st downs are generated off 3rd down conversions. The remaining 65-75% are generated on 1st and 2nd downs.

In 1994, the Vikings ranked 3rd in the NFL in generating 1st downs. Of the 325 1st downs we achieved, 99 came on 3rd downs, while 226 were generated on 1st and 2nd downs. In 1995, we produced 342 1st downs: 114 on 3rd downs, and 228 on 1st or 2nd downs.

	EARNED 1ST DOWN	3RD DOWN CONV	%	1ST/2ND CONV	%
MINNESOTA	342	114	33%	228	67%
DENVER	344	89	26%	255	74%
CHICAGO	340	88	26%	252	74%
GREEN BAY	339	108	32%	321	68%
PITTSBURGH	394	97	25%	297	75%
SAN DIEGO	314	95	30%	219	70%
WASHINGTON	297	98	33%	199	67%

This is why the 3rd down conversion, however important, has never been one of the top measurable categories of probability that were discussed earlier in this book.

A secondary objective for your 1st and 2nd down calls is to make sure to leave yourself in as short a 3rd down situation as possible. As we can see in the 3rd down section of this book, your chances of conversion on 3rd down nearly doubles from 3rd and long to 3rd and medium to 3rd and short. Elements of your play selection should emphasize the +4 yards efficiency on 1st and 2nd down that was discussed earlier.

The final priority should be a conscious effort to produce an explosive play. We documented earlier the importance that explosive plays have on the probability of winning, either through scoring or with huge shifts in field position.

First and 2nd down are the best chances you have for creating explosive plays because of the multiple concerns that defenses must prepare for. If you are creating explosive plays as a basic part of your route progression, or if you have had a couple of broken tackles for big gains, this will suffice.

However, if you have gone a couple of series of four, five, or six plays without creating an explosive play, then create one. In 1995, the Vikings led the NFL in 5-minute drives and was second in 10-play drives. Yet, at its best you are going to only be able to do this less than 20% of the time. The league average was even more diffi-

	TOTAL 1ST DOWN	5 MIN. DRIVES	%
MINNESOTA	196	32	16%
CHICAGO	175	27	15%
PITTSBURGH	193	26	13%
SAN DIEGO	177	23	13%
GREEN BAY	180	23	13%
DENVER	181	22	12%
WASHINGTON	185	14	8%

cult, with teams producing 10-play drives only 11% (22/188) of the time.

The route combinations in our opening examples (although a very simplistic approach) show how you might tie your formation and plays together with the three priorities in mind. Most of the combinations , given the right defenses, present an opportunity to get a big play down the field or get the 1st down, with some type of

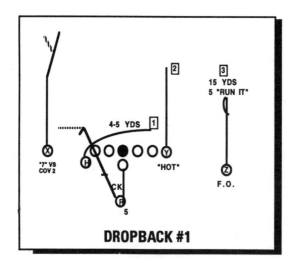

DROPBACK #1

underneath route to maintain the +4 yard average.

The play illustrated in Dropback #1 is a good example of the different priorities you can use in designing your opening sequences. For example, this play gives you a chance to hit X on the skinny post for an "explosion" if you get some form of man free or three deep. On the other hand, if the defense rolls its coverage to the weak side, you have a chance to get the first down with the 5 route of the Z receiver. The drop off routes to the H and R are also high percentage throws that should maintain your +4 yards efficiency objective.

Summary
The key elements in establishing your base offense are:

1)   *Determine the size and scope* of the package you need.
2)   Determine if there is a recognizable *difference* between *1st down and 2nd long.*
3)   *Establish* an *opening sequence* and be specific with regard to what you want to run and why—then *stick by it.*
4)   Keep your *opening sequences interactive* with regard to *personnel and formations.*
5)   Keep your *opening priorities* in mind:
     • *Get a 1st down*
     • Keep yourself in a convertible 3rd down distance
     • Create an "explosive"

CHAPTER 3

3rd Down

As was mentioned in the previous chapter on base offense, the third down offense is obviously a critical situation. Even though the 25-35% of 1st downs generated in this situation are not proportionally as large a part of your total game plan, the significance of maintaining a drive and having three more chances to advance the ball are evident.

As we have done previously, let's first examine the scope of the situation. The last four years the average NFL team faced 3rd down situations between 215-220 times a year. The distances involved in these circumstances break down roughly like this:

OVERALL:	AVG	PER
3RD 11+	32	2.0
3RD 7-10	64	4.0
3RD 4-6	48	3.0
3RD 2-3	48	3.0
3RD 1	24	1.5
	216	13.5

These figures can vary for you depending upon your level. Most high school teams are not in the Red Zone as much as college and professional teams. As a result, they don't face as many 3rd and longs due to the proportionately lower number of plays that are run. However, the ratios will stay amazingly similar.

Broken down between Open Field and Red Zone, the numbers look like this:

OPEN FIELD:	AVG	PER
3RD 11+	16	1.0
3RD 7-10	48	3.0
3RD 4-6	32	2.0
3RD 2-3	32	2.0
3RD 1	16	1.0
RED ZONE		
3RD 11+	16	1.0
3RD 7-10	16	1.0
3RD 4-6	16	1.0
3RD 2-3	16	1.0
3RD 1	8	0.5
	216	13.5

The aforementioned numbers reflect the ratios we faced the last two years with the Vikings. As was mentioned earlier, we face a high number of third down situations due to the nature of our offense and our productivity level on 1st and 2nd downs:

Open Field:	1994	1995	Avg	Per
3RD 11+	26	30	28	1.75
3RD 7-10	66	55	61	3.78
3RD 4-6	35	46	41	2.53
3RD 2-3	30	20	25	1.56
3RD 1	17	22	20	1.22
Red Zone:				
3RD 11+	4	12	8	0.50
3RD 7-10	28	15	22	1.34
3RD 4-6	5	16	11	0.66
3RD 2-3	16	14	15	0.94
3RD 1	8	11	10	0.59
	235	241	238	15

This section will concentrate on the 3rd down package in the Open Field. The third downs faced in the Red Zone will be discussed in the Red Zone Chapter.

I find this part of the game plan, however critical, one of the easiest to prepare for because the amount of offense needed is so specific and identifiable.

Our 3rd down package has been very successful the last two years with our 47.7% conversion in 1995 being the 5th highest conversion rate in the NFL for the last five years. No team in the NFL has converted more 3rd downs the last two seasons.

The Vikings' third-down conversion numbers for the last four years were as follows:

3RD DOWN CONVERSIONS					
OPEN FIELD:	1992	1993	1994	1995	AVG
3RD 1					
ATT.	27	16	17	22	21
MADE	16	10	11	20	14
%	59%	63%	65%	91%	70%
3RD 2-3					
ATT.	30	26	33	20	27
MADE	18	13	18	15	16
%	60%	50%	55%	75%	59%
3RD 4-6					
ATT.	42	33	35	46	39
MADE	20	16	13	24	18
%	48%	48%	37%	52%	47%
3RD 7-10					
ATT.	51	48	66	55	55
MADE	11	11	27	13	16
%	22%	23%	41%	24%	28%
3RD 11+					
ATT.	24	33	26	30	28
MADE	3	5	4	8	5
%	13%	15%	15%	27%	18%
TOTAL ATT.	174	156	177	173	170
TOTAL MADE	68	55	73	80	69
TOTAL %	39%	35%	41%	46%	41%

The average team in the NFL will convert 38-40% of its 3rd down attempts. The highest conversion rate in the NFL in 1995 was 50% by the Green Bay Packers.

The percentage of success increases substantially as the distance decreases:

      3rd and Long   20-25%
      3rd and Medium 45-50%
      3rd and Short   75-85%

These percentages underline the importance of maintaining a 1st/2nd +4 efficiency that enhances your chances of keeping your 3rd down calls in at least the 50%+ region.

3rd and Long

3rd and long is any distance greater than +7 yards. By virtue of the distance needed, this is obviously the most difficult area to convert. There are two basic approaches you can take in this down and distance situation: 1) go for the total distance with a throw down the field; or 2) drop or hand the ball off underneath and give a player a chance to get the distance needed in the open field.

Although the effect on you between a 3rd and 7-10 and a 3rd and 11+ situation may involve facing and reacting to a different defense, it usually just involves an adjustment like deepening the depths of some of your individual routes due the extra distance required for a 1st down.

We usually script five passes for this situation, not including whatever base draws or traps we have scheduled for Nickel runs. We also always have some form of screen in this situation that is not part of the five throws.

Most defensive teams tend to do one of two things in this long distance situation: 1) they will either play whatever form of passive zone package they have, emphasizing the importance of keeping the ball in front of them and driving on the underneath route; or 2) they will pressure you, hoping to force a break off route or a dump pass to a "hot" back that even if completed usually falls short of the distance needed for the 1st down.

Of these two scenarios, the former is the most dangerous for the offense. One of the hardest things to do is to get a quarterback to not force the ball into a loaded zone in hopes of making a big play. Knowing when and where to take a chance, and when to drop the ball off and play the percentages is the surest sign of measuring a quarterback's maturity. This is the ultimate test of how far the "umbilical cord" between you and the quarterback can stretch.

As a coach, you have to understand that coaching can take the player only so far and that at some point either he is capable of making the right decision and executing the play or he isn't.

As a coach all you can do is lay out and practice the anticipated coverages you will see and make sure the quarterback knows when the percentages are on his side or not. As we mentioned earlier, if you provide as much "information" as you can to the quarterback, you can "reduce his level of uncertainty".

One of the keys to this is educating the quarterback and the team that a 1-in-4 conversion rate in long yardage situation (7+) is a very successful ratio. A 2-of-5 conversion rate will put you way ahead of the curve.

Screens and draws can occasionally catch a defense off guard. Such a scenario, however, is difficult to accomplish with any real consistency. Screens and draws also present an excellent way to simply get out of a series, punt the ball and start over.

Certainly, times exist when discretion is the better part of valor. Something can be said, however, for having a positive offensive gain on third down even though it does not convert. Taking a sack, throwing an interception (even if it is 40 yards down the field), or just arbitrarily throwing the ball down the field can have a very strong negative effect on the mental state of our team—particularly our offense.

A yardage gain that just doesn't quite get there can still be viewed in a positive manner by the offense and give you something to build on. In addition, it may also give you just enough yardage to affect your field position for the next series.

Each of the five passes you have scripted for this situation should have clearly defined objectives that do one or more of the following:

1)   Given the right rotation by the secondary, gives you a deep throw down the field for a substantial gain.
2)   If given the right one-on-one match up, allows your receiver to run a good route whereby the catch should, at a minimum, give you the yards needed for the first down.
3)   Gives the quarterback, by way of a dump-off or primary receiver, a receiver who has a chance to make an easy catch (preferably facing the defense), allowing him to try to make a move that will give him the distance needed after the catch.

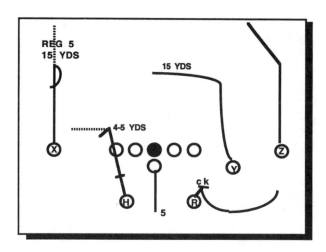

In this progression we have the potential for a deep throw down the middle of the field should the defense decide to play a flat "0" coverage with no free safety in the middle of the field, or perhaps a "$\frac{1}{4}$-$\frac{1}{4}$" halves coverage where the $\frac{1}{4}$ strong safety gets pulled up by the inside route of the Y receiver.

If the defense sits in a loose cover 2, there is an opportunity to find a window to the inside route by the Y receivers, hopefully at the first down depth.

If the defense sits in a form of three deep or man free, you may have a chance to work the backside 5 route if you like the matchup with your X receiver and the left cornerback. If you are going to use this route in both 3rd and long situations, you may want to deepen the depth of the 5 route to 18 yards.

If the quarterback is forced to dump the ball to the swing receiver (R), at least the back is moving down field and may have the chance to make a move and get the first down.

Forcing a "hot" throw or "break off" can be an effective tactic by the defense but carries great risk. If a team does this, it will be one of two forms: 1) a zone dog/blitz with pressure coming from one side or the other accompanied by zone coverage behind it, or 2) a more aggressive dog/blitz with increased pressure, possibly from both sides, and man coverage behind it. This is an area where your quarterback must have a thorough knowledge of his protection schemes. If it is a zone dog/blitz and they have not brought sufficient people from the correct side to pressure you, the quarterback must not panic and force the ball too quickly if he indeed has adequate protection to pick up the pressure.

On the other hand, if the pressure presents him with a free rusher, he must be fully aware of his vulnerability and have been schooled on what his options are at that point.

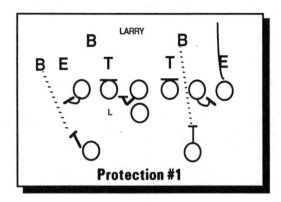

Protection #1

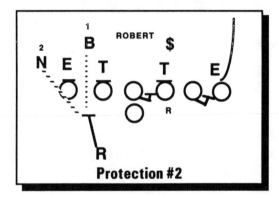

Protection #2

A four-man weakside dog is a typical situation the quarterback must be ready to face.

Protection #1 is a 7 man-based protection scheme that has no problem picking up the 4th defender from the weak side. Protection #2 is a 6 man-based scheme with the center committed to the strong side. If you are not able to redirect the center to the four-man side, the quarterback must be prepared to hit a "hot" or "break off" receiver if both the linebackers come.

Few teams do this type of blitzing arbitrarily. If they show a history of zone/blitz or total pressure, you must make sure your quarterback is aware of his options with every route that is installed.

Again, remember that an effective "hot" or "break off" route , even if it doesn't achieve the first down, is far preferable to the quarterback getting sacked and maybe even fumbling.

A run in this down and distance is worth a shot particularly if you keep the 1-in-4 ratio in mind and have already converted on one 3rd and Long.

The NFL average for runs in this situation was only 11 per team a year, converting on two. The team with the most 3rd and 7+ run conversions in 1995 was Jacksonville with seven conversions in 17 attempts.

I offer one additional note in this situation. I often see teams making a deep play fake to an I back on 3rd and Long. I understand that some teams may only have a certain route combination tied to that protection scheme, usually some form of a turnback zone. If you are not willing to carry additional protection and drop the quarterback straight back, at least school the quarterback to take a drop with the turnback protection that allows him to abandon the fake in this situation.

I understand play action fakes can be helpful, but in this down and distance, I doubt you are going to fool anyone. As a result, you should never make the quarterback take his eyes off coverage rotation unless a play fake is going to substantially help the route.

3rd and Medium
This is made up of both the 3rd and 2-3 and 3rd and 4-6 package. Both are separate and distinct packages. The major difference between the two situations lies in the ability of a run to get the yardage needed. We will usually carry a total of six plays in 3rd and medium, four in 3rd and 4-6, and two in 3rd and 2-3.

Conversions on 3rd and medium are absolutely critical because of the effect they have on our play-calling mentality. If you are confident and successful in this situation, your 1st and 2nd down calls can take on a whole added dimension knowing that you can convert a majority of your 3rd and mediums. This may allow you to take more chances at verticals on 1st down knowing that all you have to do with your 2nd down call is get to a 3rd and medium, or you may be willing to do more with your 2nd and medium plays knowing you are already in a high-percentage 3rd down situation. On the other hand, if your 3rd and medium offense does not have a substantially higher success ratio than does your 3rd and long, you are less apt to stay with the run on 2nd and long and will lose much of the balance so many teams strive to achieve.

In a 3rd and 4-6 situation, a run other than a draw or a trap is hard to consistently get the full 4-6 yards. Keep in mind the best of running teams over the last four years in the NFL have averaged just one run a game in 3rd and anything over two yards. Even with this in mind, it is always one of our goals to get at least one run a game in a true 3rd down and medium to long situation.

Play action passes become legitimate fakes in this down and distance situation, particularly as the distance needed decreases. It is important that you use play fakes that are tied to runs. Our runs in this situation are most always draws or traps, so our play action series consists of fake draws or our fake trap series.

This is also an area where we take special care to match the plays up by formation and personnel. We often use a series of shift and motions on two or three of the plays with very different routes on each play. Also, we prefer not to run plays here that have been used earlier in the game. If we are using a base combination that we use a lot in 1st and 2nd down, we will wait until we have used it in this situation before we go back to using it in the normal down and distance situation.

The following three diagrams illustrate the play progression of some route combinations that are run by many teams in the League:

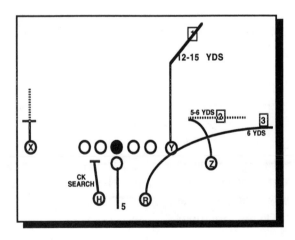

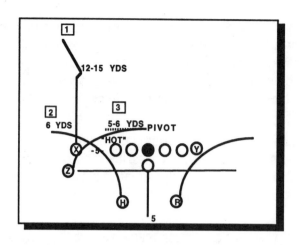

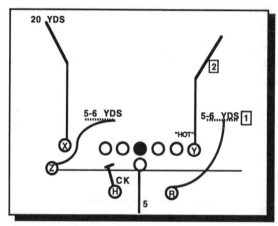

We usually include a quick hitch out in this area, either as a primary or a backside route. Many times this simple and efficient play can get the desired results.

Run Play Action FROM TRIANGLES GO FOR THE TD CORNER RT. THIS WILL KEEP THEM ON THEIR HEELS

3rd and Short

The most important thing to remember in a 3rd and 1 situation is that you are usually in this situation only one time a game. This certainly doesn't mean you need carry only one play in your game plan. On the other hand, I often see people list eight and nine plays in this situation.

Two trains of thought exist regarding this down and distance situation: 1) get the first down, or 2) take a shot at a big play.

The conversion rate for this situation is not as high as you would think. The average conversion rate of the NFL the last four years is around 65-70%. In 1995 we led the NFL in 3rd and 1 conversions converting 30 of 36 attempts (83 %). That figure jumped to 91% percent in the open field.

Our run/pass ratio in a 3rd and short situation looked like this:

20 of 23 runs
10 of 13 passes

Our basic approach was to run the ball from three separate personnel groupings each game. We carried a three tight end (Jumbo) smash ball play, a normal two-back or two-tights play, and spread the defense with a 3 or 4 wide personnel formation.

The last three years, the teams that have had the highest conversion rate used just a quarterback wedge to gain the 1st down many times.

Occasionally a team will cover off your center and both guards and even pepper one or more linebackers into the gaps. For this purpose, you must have an audible ready to take advantage of the other vulnerabilities a defense who commits to this type of alignment will present to you.

If you decide to carry a play with "big play" or TD potential, be certain that it is just that, a big play. You would hate to take the chance of passing up the high percentage 3rd and 1 run for a "big play" that only gets 5-10 yards.

Your Jumbo formation is probably the best formation with which to break a big play. A play action fake over your best blockers with your best back, particularly in a critical situation, is your best chance of bringing the secondary up into the position you want.

Keep in mind that you are usually only going to be in this situation once a game, so you may practice this "big" play every week for six weeks and never use it. However, the repetitions you have put into this play may pay big dividends when you need them the most.

Given the nature of your level of play, you may find you are in more 3rd or 4th and 1 situations. You may, because of your lack of a kicking game, be in more four down situations where you are willing to go for it more on a 4th and 1 situation than is typically seen on the professional level. As with any situation, you need to determine what you will need to win the game and how committed you are to going for it. These are decisions that should be made during the week and not during the "heat of battle" on game day.

Summary

The key elements in establishing your 3rd down package are:

1)   Determine the *size and scope* of your package.

2)   Recognize the *success ratio* you can expect in each phase:

> *3rd and Long*   *20-25%*
> *3rd and Medium 45-50%*
> *3rd and Short*   *75-85%*

3)   Leave your *options* open for your quarterback and be certain he *understands what those options are.*

4)   Have a *plan* to handle the *blitz.*

5)   Match your *plays* by *personnel and formation.*

6)   *Determine* your plan for 3rd and *short* during the week and *stay with your plan.*

CHAPTER 4

Pre-Red Zone

No one questions the fact that the Red Zone and efficiency in the Red Zone are vitally important to winning any game. However, an area many game plans don't adequately account for is the part of the field leading up to the Red Zone. This Pre-Red Zone offense is particularly important if you have a field goal kicker who has an effective range from at least 20 to 30 yards. We are very fortunate to have Fuad Reveiz as our field goal kicker. Fuad has proven to be extremely accurate from the 30-yard line in. As evidence of his accuracy, Fuad holds the NFL record with 30 consecutive field goals.

Given Fuad's exceptional skills, coupled with the importance of Red Zone efficiency, we established the Pre-Red Zone area as a critical area of our situational game plan. We know that once we get past the 30-yard line, we have a very high degree of success in getting at least three points.

The priority for us once we cross the 50-yard line is to use a combination of plays that increase our chances of crossing the 30-yard line. We accomplish this in two ways: 1) utilizing plays that have the highest degree of success in the 10-15-yard range, and 2) though you do not want to become too conservative in your approach, avoid plays that might put your team in a position where they have to convert a 3rd and Long just to get into scoring position. To accomplish this, we take special care not to run plays that have the potential for a big loss (reverses or sweeps) or protections that have the quarterback sit deep in the pocket making a lot of reads. This is an excellent place on the field to run your quick passing game or rollouts by the quarterback.

If you do not have a kicker with the type of consistency that we are given by Fuad, your Pre-Red Zone approach takes on a whole different perspective. The closer you get to the Red Zone, the harder it becomes to just physically overwhelm your opponent and push the ball in for the score. Likewise, the passing lanes become tighter and tighter with every yard as you approach the end zone. For this reason, you may need to use the Pre-Red Zone area as a place to take a high number of vertical shots. It is also a place you may want to run your specials.

In both instances, whether you are simply focusing on getting the ball inside the 30-yard line or taking extra vertical shots, you will want to establish a three- or four-play progression covering the objectives you set for your team.

It is important that you make your team aware of the priorities you are setting in this area so that your quarterback knows what is expected of him in this situation, and how many risks he may want to take.

This is also, based on your kicking capabilities, an area to determine how far out you will extend your 4th down territory. This is something that should be planned for during the week and explained to your players. If you go for a 4th down and have not made your team aware of your intentions to do so earlier, they may misinterpret your actions as evidence of panic on your part.

CHAPTER 5

Red Zone

Along with the conversion of 3rd downs, the Red Zone is clearly the most critical situation the offense will be in during the course of a game.

Like 3rd down, the size and scope of the Red Zone can be very specifically defined. This area is actually divided into three distinct areas: Red Zone, +10 and goal line.

The last four years the average team in the NFL has had 45-50 series a season in the Red Zone and has converted its Red Zone possessions to points between 80-85% of the time. This averages out to about three Red Zone possessions a game.

The following chart illustrates how often selected NFL teams found themselves in the Red Zone:

RED ZONE:	MINN	DENVER	CHICAGO	GREEN BAY	PITTS	SAN DIEGO	WASH	TEAM AVG	PER GAME AVG
1ST DOWN	78	63	79	74	75	63	74	72	4.5
2ND LONG	50	37	43	44	51	43	57	45	2.8
2ND MED	45	35	48	31	40	23	30	36	2.3
2ND 1	7	10	7	6	10	7	6	8	0.5
3RD 11+	12	3	1	1	9	12	7	6	0.4
3RD 7-10	15	16	19	17	24	16	19	18	1.1
3RD 4-6	16	17	24	13	18	8	18	16	1.0
3RD 2-3	14	9	6	19	8	15	17	13	0.8
3RD 1	11	11	10	7	5	4	5	8	0.5
4TH	7	6	9	3	16	6	10	8	0.5
1ST GOAL	24	28	45	30	35	23	25	30	1.9
									16.3

The last two years, for example, the Minnesota Vikings had 54 and 57 Red Zone possessions, respectively.

Our Red Zone down and distance distribution looked like this:

RED ZONE:	1992	1993	1994	1995	AVG	PER
1ST SERIES	9	7	4	12	8	0.50
1ST 10+	2	1	4	3	3	0.16
1ST EARNED	60	51	70	63	61	3.81
1ST GOAL	25	26	20	24	24	1.48
2ND LONG	41	44	52	50	47	2.92
2ND MED	26	27	29	45	32	1.98
2ND 1	13	8	6	7	9	0.53
3RD 11+	7	3	4	12	7	0.41
3RD 7-10	10	18	28	15	18	1.11
3RD 4-6	11	17	5	16	12	0.77
3RD 2-3	13	10	16	14	13	0.83
3RD 1	10	9	8	11	10	0.59
4TH	4	1	9	7	5	0.33

Earlier we discussed the importance of Red Zone efficiency and how it was one of the top four in measurable probability with respect to winning a game. Our contrast in Red Zone efficiency from 1993 to 1994 was a case study in the importance of Red Zone efficiency.

We previously mentioned about the limitations on our offense in 1993 compared to the production in 1994 when we set the all-time total offensive yardage mark. In 1993, we had 45 Red Zone possessions and scored 43 times for a 96% conversion rate. That percentage led the league in 1993.

In 1994, we were a good deal more productive and had 54 Red Zone possessions but had only 44 scores, falling back to the League average of 80%. Had we maintained our 90%+ efficiency rating in 1994, we would have scored 400+ points. During the 1995 season, our Red Zone efficiency improved to the point where we broke the Minnesota Vikings' all-time seasonal scoring record for 412 points.

Given these parameters, we carry approximately 10 plays (five runs and five passes) for 1st and 2nd down in the Red Zone. We also carry two plays for 3rd and long and 3rd and medium. Our 3rd and 1 play will usually carry over from the open field. We also carry three or four "end zone" plays that will be prioritized by field position (+25 to +15, +15 to +10, +10 to +5).

More and more teams are playing a loose 4-across zone concept inside the Red Zone. The result is that there are fewer of the man-for-man match ups that made pick routes very prominent in years past. This zone concept puts a higher priority on being able to run the ball effectively and hitting underneath routes that (hopefully) enable receivers to score after catching the ball.

Three of the top four teams in touchdown efficiency in the League in 1995 were Philadelphia, Dallas and Seattle—not surprisingly, who were also three of the top rushing teams in the NFL.

Mention was made earlier about the Pre-Red Zone area and the priority of getting into scoring position. Whatever the range of your field goal kicker is, it is important that once you get inside that range you minimize the chance of being pushed back out of that area.

Once we cross the 30-yard line we are very careful to not run plays that carry the potential for a loss that would take us out of field goal range. This means avoid calling deep drop routes or special plays that could result in losing yards out of this area. Once we cross the 20-yard line, we are less concerned with the depth of our drops causing a sack which might keep us out of field goal range.

Defenses tend to begin their Red Zone packages at different places from the +20 to the +10. Teams tend to be very specific about what they will run vs. different personnel groupings. Lawyers have a saying, "Don't ask a question you don't already know the answer to". This is very valuable advice. Be very hesitant to introduce a personnel or formation groupings to which you don't have a pretty good idea of how the defense is going to react. This is no place to surprise your quarterback.

The Red Zone is also an excellent place for different plays from formations you may have run in the open field. This will cause hesitation in a defense when it thinks it has seen something before and you run counter to that.

+10
In 1995 the average team in the NFL had 26 1st-and-goal-to-go series. The better teams in the league will usually have between 35-40 series in this area. In either case you should plan for about two series a game in this area. The size of the amount of offense we will need here each week suggests that you have a specific plan for your two or three runs in this area, and base one or two passes off of those formations.

This close to the goal line every pass is virtually a shot for the end zone so the quarterback must be very focused on what he expects to see before he throws the ball. This is an area in which it is very hard to account for everyone, which makes the quarterback vulnerable to being intercepted. Nothing will demoralize an offense more than to move the ball the length of the field, then to turn the ball over so close to scoring.

Goal Line

Like your short yardage offense, this is an area in which is easy to carry too much offense into the game plan.

In 1995, the average NFL team ran three plays a game in this situation. Our ratio over the last four years looked like this:

	1992	1993	1994	1995	AVG	PER
GOAL LINE	34	35	41	36	37	2.3

Recognize that you will rarely run more than three or four goal line plays. You will rarely need more than three runs and one play action off your primary formation here.

You can always use one of your +10 plays or one of your 2 point plays.

2-Point Plays

Now that the NFL has adopted the 2-point rule, we have come in alignment with high school and college play sequencing. There are two major differences in the NFL:

- Our 2-point line is at the 2-yard line, making the run much more viable.

- With the possibility of overtime, the use of two points, particularly at the end of a game, is substantially less critical. The NCAA has just recently changed the Division 1A rule to allow for overtime.

Most teams averaged only one 2-point play a year, with the highest number being five attempts by the Arizona Cardinals. This is down from the previous year, where the league averaged two 2-point attempts a year.

We normally carry three 2-point plays into most games. While this number is extremely high given the number of 2-point plays actually run, we pointed out earlier that it is also a way to expand your goal line offense. As a result, our actions have a lot of carryover value.

Most of our 2-point plays are run out of our regular and the 3 wides personnel alignments. As a result, this setup also serves as a contrast of choices to your normal goal line offense, which utilizes three tight ends.

Regarding 2-point plays, one of the major coaching points for your quarterback is to remember that an interception can not be returned for any points on 2-point attempts. For this reason, he should go down fighting and if all else appears lost, just throw the ball up for grabs if there is no clear place to go. This certainly differs from a 3rd down attempt made from the same area, where the option of kicking a field goal is still available or if it is 4th down, a "lost" ball can be returned by the defense for points. This rule differs in the college game where the defense can return a 2-point conversion for an equal number of points.

Summary

The key elements in establishing your Red Zone package are:

1) Determine the *size and scope* of your package.

2) Determine the *abilities of your kicking game* and once inside field goal range, *never* put yourself in position to be *taken out of that range.*

3) Eliminate as many "surprises" in your offensive plan for the Red Zone as you can; this is an area where you must have the most detailed part of your game plan.

4) Coordinate your +10, Goal Line, and 2-point plan to be *interactive.* Be prepared to carry one aspect of the plan into the other.

CHAPTER 6

Special Categories

This section of the book examines the special categories that do not take up a substantial percentage of your game plan. In some instances, these situations may not even come up in a game. When they do come up, however, they can be critical to the outcome of a game.

These special category areas include:

- Backed up offense
- Special 1st-down plays
- Blitz situations
- 2-minute offense
- 4-minute offense
- Last three plays of the game/half

Backed Up Offense

Teams in the NFL are not backed up on their goal line as much as high school or college teams are. Regardless of the level at which you are coaching, however, you must have an adequate offensive package ready for this situation.

We basically prepare one offensive series for our backed up offensive needs.

The goal for this situation is obvious: get at least one 1st down. At this point, the opponent's goal line looks a million miles away and the offense may feel a little pressured.

It is important to focus the offensive team on the most immediate task at hand. The intermediate goal of getting one 1st down will allow them to focus on a much less imposing chore.

If the ball is literally backed up to the goal line, your linemen must be even more aware of their splits, and the players handling the ball must take extra care. We carry two base plays in this situation and an additional 3rd and medium and 3rd and long call. These plays are base calls that we are very familiar with and in which the players have a great deal of confidence. Although they are base plays, that does not mean they have to be the most conservative plays in the playbook.

Bobby Bowden, the extremely successful coach at Florida State, gave a clinic speech on backed up offense aptly named, "Hang loose, one of us is fixing to score!" This is an excellent approach to take in this situation. If you are unable to get the 1st down and get out from under the shadow of your goal post, the chances are very good your opponent will convert this opportunity into some form of points.

If you are willing to throw the ball in this situation, you have a relatively good chance to hit something down the field since most defenses tend to play fairly conservatively in this situation. It is important that your quarterback knows what is expected of him and what he should do based on the expected fronts and coverages.

Keep in mind that this situation can turn into a real positive for your offense. It is very demoralizing for a defense when they let an offense out of this situation. If you are able to get a 1st down, the next play is an excellent time to take a shot down the field.

Special 1st Down Plays

This part of your special categories covers two plays: 1st down and less than 10 and 1st down and more than 10.

The 1st and less than 10 situation is usually a 1st and 5 due to an offsides penalty called on the defense. Most teams in the NFL face this situation only a few times a year. Frankly, I don't imagine it happens much more at the high school or collegiate levels.

Still, you want to be prepared with a call. Many people will use this as a chance to take a shot at a big play, figuring they are already at 2nd and medium at worst. The only problem with this philosophy is the defense is usually thinking the same thing and is probably in a mode that will make a big play even harder to do.

What you can accomplish is running a play that sets up a big play down the road, or calling a play that runs counter to something you run a lot or have already run. Although getting a true "explosive" may be harder to accomplish, a good solid 10-yard gain is always welcome yardage. Of course, taking advantage of the situation to just pound out another 1st down is not the worst train of thought either.

First and 10+ unfortunately happens with much more frequency during a game and is something that must be a part of every game plan. This occurs, on the average, once a game—much more frequently than does 1st and less than 10.

The key to this situation is to recognize that a legitimate priority is to just get back to 2nd and 10 or better. Third and 11+ is the longest odds you will face in any situation in football and should be avoided at all cost. It is no surprise that the NFL teams who have faced the most 3rd and 11+ situations a year are the same teams with the worst 3rd down conversion rates.

With this in mind, you must school your team to understand the importance of getting back to a respectable 2nd-down distance. You can help your team by properly analyzing what the defense will probably do in this situation. This situation usually comes up after an illegal procedure call on the offense or a holding call. In your weekly preparation, it is important to analyze if a defense has a pattern to what they do in either situation, and if each situation elicits a separate tendency by the defense.

This is one of those situations that, numerically, is so small it is easy to package and prepare your team to face. Like all our offensive situations, if you can accurately predict what the defense will do in this very specific circumstance, your team should have a great deal of confidence knowing the play they are running is designed for this specific situation.

The play you call certainly does not have to be a special play or anything you don't normally run. On the contrary, it should be something your team is very comfortable with and has experienced a reasonable amount of success using.

Blitz Situations

In 1994 and 1995, teams in the NFL faced a true blitz situation a little over a 100 times a year. This total averages out to about 6-7 blitzes per game per team.

The NFL keeps track of how each team does by assigning percentages to attempts vs. completions, yards gained, touchdowns or turnovers, and sack ratio. By assigning these totals, a rating (much like the quarterback rating the league uses to make their quarterback rankings), the NFL ranks each team on its ability to handle the blitz.

The following chart illustrates how seven NFL teams handled the blitz (comparatively speaking) in 1995:

	ATT	COMP	YDS	TD	T.O.	SACKS	RATING
MINNESOTA	141	87	1097	11	1	10	108.97
GREEN BAY	112	66	1019	7	3	11	98.77
DENVER	92	42	646	9	3	7	93.84
CHICAGO	127	74	567	4	2	1	88.3
PITTSBURGH	115	65	866	4	3	7	80.56
SAN DIEGO	107	49	582	6	6	7	58.24
WASHINGTON	94	39	432	3	4	15	48.71

The Vikings' 108.97 rating led the NFL in 1995. In 1994, we ranked sixth in the league with an 89.9 rating.

We usually carry two or three "blitz beaters" in our game plan. These are specific plays (protections) that can be called or audibled to take advantage of specific pressure defenses.

Most pressure fronts can be handled with your basic plays by hitting a hot route or in some instances by redirecting the run. If there is a specific pressure package you are worried about, or there is one that you think presents an opportunity to hit a big play, this is the instance you are looking for to use your "blitz beaters". A blitz beater could be something as simple as a quick slant or a more elaborate 8-man protection scheme with a throw down the field. In either case, it is important that your team know what your objective is in using this play and when you expect to go to it.

This is a part of your game plan that mentally and emotionally must be addressed with your team. We have always taken the approach that the blitz is an "opportunity" rather than something that should be feared. We stress that a blitz is a chance to make a big play or create one of the "explosives" we are consistently trying to run.

Be careful about relying on an 8-man protection scheme as the basis of your blitz beaters. Often this is something that a team will spend a great deal of time on and yet only use a few times a year. If an eight-man protection scheme is only something that you audible to in extreme situations, it is not something you are going to execute with a great deal of confidence.

If you can put a viable package together that is more a part of your base offense and is something you do on a more regular basis, it will increase your chances of success a great deal. Keep in mind that if a team is committed to the blitz, like former Arizona Cardinals coach Buddy Ryan's package, then you must obviously expand your blitz package. In fact, you should make it the basis of your game plan that week.

Two-Minute Offense

The two-minute offense is a very challenging, yet exciting, part of any game. It is an area of the offense that must be practiced each week. Furthermore, your two-minute offense should have a very specific structure with regard to procedures and plays.

Every player, not just the quarterback, must be aware of the rules that affect any two-minute situation, most importantly what affects the game clock. A multitude of "clock" situations exist that could affect this period. Nothing looks worse than to see a team staring at each other during this time period, wondering whether they should huddle or use a no-huddle offense. It is hard to make them aware of every situation. We subscribe to the general rule:

> ## WHAT STOPS THE CLOCK-STARTS THE CLOCK!

What this rule encompasses is the concept that if the officials stop the play, then the officials will spot the ball and play will resume immediately. On the other hand, if the ball stops the play (incomplete pass or run out of bounds), then it takes the next snap of the ball to start the clock and you have time to huddle.

Most offenses have a no-huddle offense for this part of their game plan. In addition, it is a good time to have and practice a two-play sequence, (i.e., calling two plays in the huddle). Such a sequence is particularly useful inside the Red Zone.

"Killing" the clock with the spiking of the ball can be an effective tool if you have few or no time-outs. In some situations, for example—after a long gain, and if time requires it, spiking the ball on 1st down is sometimes preferable to rushing a play and being forced into a couple of critical calls which have to be made at the line.

Above all else the quarterback, and if possible the team, must be schooled as to what your objective is (touchdown or field goal), what field position is needed if you are positioning for a field goal, and what your time-out situation is. In addition, this is an aspect of the game where you as the coach must be able to take as much pressure off the quarterback as possible. A signal system should be used for the quarterback so that he can check with you on every play as to what needs to be done—run, pass or call time out.

Four-Minute Offense

This aspect of the offense is one we all like working with because it indicates we are in control of the game and are trying to run the clock out. Like the two-minute offense, it is vital that your quarterback and team know exactly what is expected during the four-minute offense, what the rules are and what plays they can anticipate being run.

One of the more common phrases used in football is, "a running clock is worth 35 seconds." Your team must remember that getting a 1st down is the second priority in this situation to the number one priority of keeping the clock running.

You should school your offense about what personnel and formation groupings will be used, especially if they are groupings that you do not use regularly or have not used a lot this game. The last thing you want to do is stop the clock because you don't have the right people on the field.

It is best that your passing offense be limited to action passes that break containment, and that the quarterback knows that incompletions are not an option here. A sack and loss of yardage is far more preferable to stopping the clock.

We carry any number of base running plays from appropriate formations that can be used during your four-minute offense. These are all usually plays that are a base part of the game plan or plays that you run every week and the players are familiar with without a lot of extra practice. If you are going to spend time in practice on your four-minute offense, you should focus on the passes you may want to use. This step will help school your quarterback in the different priorities of passing the ball in this situation.

Last Three Plays
We carry three plays for the end of the half or game that include the desperation "hail Mary" or special "flea flickers" run down the field. These plays should be practiced every week and should be run regardless if the score is 40-0 or 14-10.

Players should also be made aware that a game cannot end on a defensive penalty. Furthermore, if a field goal can win the game, your field goal team must be up and ready. This step is something that must be practiced during the week.

A final note that you should consider with regard to this situation and two-minute offense. It is obviously important that your players do not sense that you are panicked in this situation. Your confidence and poise will carry over to them. However, this is a critical situation with time being a major factor. Your normal demeanor will probably change, no matter how confident and poised you are, simply because time dictates a much more "hurried" pace. School your players about how your demeanor may change so that they do not misinterpret your change in character as a sign of panic.

Summary

The key elements in establishing your special category package are:

1) Determine *size and scope* of each package even if it is unlikely it will come up.
2) Coach your players to *understand the unique properties* of each of these situations.
3) Stress the importance of preparing for each situation; reinforce the fact that it may come down to one of these situations to *win a game.*
4) Make sure the players know your *intentions* in each of these areas and do not *misinterpret* your actions as a sign of *panic.*

CHAPTER 7

Installing the Offense

So far in this text, we have spent a good deal of time analyzing the size and scope of each of the situations for which offense must prepare. The following chart summarizes the amount of offense we have determined we need by situation.

		SCRIPT	REPEAT
BACKED UP	BASE		2
	3RD MED		1
	3RD LONG		1
OPEN FIELD	1ST DOWN	30	
	1ST 5		1
	1ST 15		1
	2ND LONG	15	
	2ND MED	7	
	2ND 1		2
	3RD LONG	5	
	3RD 4-5	4	
	3RD 2-3	2	
	3RD 1	3	
	4TH 1		1
RED ZONE	1ST DOWN	6	
	2ND DOWN	4	
	3RD MED	2	
	3RD 1		1
	4TH 1		1
	END ZONE	3	
	+10	4	
	GOAL LINE	3	
	2 POINT	3	
		91	

The scripted column represents the upper limit of plays needed for a particular situation, keeping our 25-30% overage factor in mind. The repeat column constitutes plays that will probably come from other parts of the game plan. As such, these plays don't necessarily have to be separately scripted plays. You must, however, make sure these situations are covered and everyone is aware of what is going to be run.

I am by no means suggesting you have to have 90 different play combinations. Much of what you will call will be repeated or changed subtly by formation and or personnel. These 91 plays fall within the 20-25% overage we outlined earlier.

As large as this number may seem, many teams will unknowingly carry a much higher percentage of overage, thus making the practice ratio of game plan to actual plays called even higher.

There is a certain comfort zone that all coaches can easily fall into while preparing their team. By simply loading up the game plan with a superfluous number of plays, or by practicing in a manner in which they simply run through a number of plays, coaches can fool themselves into thinking they have covered everything they can and it is now up to their players.

Keep in mind that it is very easy to oversimplify a game plan in the guise of being "fundamentally sound" or not being too "complicated" for the players. "Some coaches rely on relatively simplistic plans," says Walsh in the already-quoted article. "When their plans don't work, they say that it was the players who did not block hard enough, did not run hard enough, or just were not tough enough."

The size and complexity of any game plan and the way you install it is not the issue. What is at issue is if you as a coach have taken the time to be as detailed and specific in your game plan preparation as is needed to give your players the best chance to succeed.

Game Plan Board

To this point, an overview of what parameters should be used to determine what each offensive situation will consist of, and how much offense is needed in each situation has been provided.

The diagram on page 75 illustrates how our Game Plan Board is arranged in our offensive coaches meeting room. We fill this board as we progress through our situational discussions. This system makes it very easy to make changes, compare plays and formations and, in general, give everyone a reference point from which to check the game plan at any given time.

In the discussion on "openers" earlier in this book, the concept of the coaching staff's ability to be on top of the game plan and the sequencing of the calls as being a major reason for establishing your openers with your coaches were discussed. Using a Game Plan Board to lay out the game plan is an excellent way to achieve this.

BASE RUN	BASE PASS	2ND LONG	3RD 11+	PRED RED ZONE	+10
			3RD 7-10	RED ZONE RUN	
					GOAL
		2ND MED	3RD 4-6	RZ BASE PASS	
			3RD 2-3	RZ END ZONE	BACKED UP: 1ST DOWN: 1. 2.
	PLAY ACTION	VERTICALS			
SCREEN			NICKEL RUNS	PRESSURE/ BLITZ	3RD MED: 3RD LONG:
SPEC. RUN					
	ACTION PASS	2ND - 1	3RD - 1	RED ZONE SY	LAST 3 PLAYS
SPEC. PASS					

Game Week Time Line
The following outline illustrates how we break up our week based on a normal Sunday game:

MONDAY

11:00 a.m.	Individual coaches finish viewing and grading video.
	View film as Off/Def staff; group viewing and analysis of video.
1:00 p.m.	Staff meeting
2:00	Team meeting
	Special teams viewing
2:30	Video viewing
4:15	On field (practice)
4:45	Practice ends
	* Coaches view video independently
6:00	Dinner
	Coaches view video independently and begin their individual game plan contributions.

TUESDAY

8:00	Offense staff meets and discusses *Base Run and Protections*.
10:00	Offense line coaches begin run and protection sheets, and view SY-GL - Red Zone
	Offense staff list *Base Pass, Play Action, and Action Passes*.
11:30	Lunch , workout, misc.
2:00 p.m.	List *Nickel Pass* and *Nickel Run*.
4:00	Staff meets to list *SY-GL*
5:00	Staff begins to list *Red Zone*
6:00	Dinner
7:00	Review *Blitz*
	Finalize:
	Script board
	Scripts and cards
	Scouting report

WEDNESDAY

7:30 a.m.	Staff meeting
8:15	QB meeting
8:30	Special team meeting
9:00	Team meeting (5)
	Scouting report
	Install Base Run, Nickel Runs, and Protections
10:00	Line breaks off
	Install base pass, play action, action passes, nickel passes
10:30	Individual meetings

11:15	Walk thru
11:45	Lunch
12:45 p.m.	Individual meetings (flexible)
	Opponents' video
1:15	Meetings over
1:30	Special teams
2:00	Practice
4:15	Practice over
5:15	Coaches review practice video
	Finalize Red Zone offense
	List backed up and 4 Minute
	Review script board and prepare cards for Thursday practice

THURSDAY

7:30 a.m.	Staff meeting
8:15	QB meeting
8:30	Special team meeting
9:00	Team meeting (5)
	View practice (OL separate)
10:00	Offense together install SY-GL-Red Zone -Backed up
10:30	Individual meeting (opponent film)
11:15	Walk thru
11:45	Lunch
12:45 p.m.	Individual meetings (flexible)
	Opponents' video
1:30	Special teams
2:00	Practice
4:15	Practice over
5:00	Coaches review practice video
	List openers
	Review script board and prepare cards for Friday practice, prepare scripts

FRIDAY

7:30 a.m.	Staff meeting
8:15	QB meeting
8:30	Special team meeting
9:00	Team meeting (5)
	Review practice video : OL separate
9:45	Offense review check and alerts
10:00	Individual meetings
11:00	Practice
1:00 p.m.	Practice over
	Finalize offensive sideline sheet

SATURDAY

9:00 a.m.	Review practice video : O.L. separate
	Individual meetings
10:30	Practice
11:15	Practice over
6:00 - 8:00 p.m.	Check into hotel
9:00 p.m.	Special teams meetings
9:30	Off/def meetings
	Use cut ups to support opening calls
	View game video to give players flavor of game plan and opponent's approach.
10:00	Team meeting
10:05	Snack

Practice Structure

The next step is to take a look at what we can realistically expect to practice in each situation and how best to proportion each section. To do this, we must first understand that there are very specific limits to the number of plays you can expect to efficiently practice in a given week.

The best way to examine this is to evaluate several key factors:

- Length of your practice
- How are your practices divided between periods (individual, group, skeleton, and team)?
- What aspect of the offense is practiced in each period?

You would expect that the overall practice time is divided up proportionately by the amount of offense used per situation. In reality, this proportion may not reflect the exact relationship to game calls, because certain situations are emphasized in a game more than others (i.e., Red Zone and 3rd downs vs. base open field offense).

If you do not identify each group/team period as a specific situation, I strongly suggest you do so. This step will help you to isolate exactly how much time you are spending in each area, and it helps the coaches and players focus on what is being called by situation.

Whatever your particular practice structure consists of, it should be easy for you to look at that structure and determine how much time is being spent in group or team situations and how it should be broken down.

As I have pointed out several times already, I am not advocating that only one way exists to set up a practice structure or that it should be a specific ratio. It is your job as a coach to determine what best suits your needs and how much attention any offensive situational segment should get. What I am advocating is that you should give substantial thought to what your particular offensive needs are and how you are you going to utilize each minute of your practice to meet those needs.

The Vikings' practice week breaks down by situations as follows:

PRACTICE RATIO

DAY	PERIOD	BASE	3RD LONG	3RD MED	SY	BU	RED ZONE	GL	2PT	TOTAL	
WEDNESDAY	W.T.	10	3	3						16	
	INSIDE	6								6	
	TEAM	8								8	
	SKEL	6		4						10	
	TEAM	6	4							10	[50]
THURSDAY	W.T.	4			2	3	5	4	2	20	
	TEAM				2		5	4	2	13	
	SKELL	6	4				4			14	
	TEAM	7		4						11	[58]
FRIDAY	TEAM				2		5	3	2	12	
	SKELL		4				6			10	[22]
TOTALS		53	15	11	6	3	25	11	6	130	
		41%	12%	8%	5%	2%	19%	8%	5%		

These numbers represent any scripted period against a live defense. What is not shown here are individual and group periods where we will service ourselves. "W.T." is a walk through period we do in shorts. The small number of snaps on Friday is due to the fact that during this practice, we use a team period to run a live two-minute drill and a separate team period to run a semi-live "move the ball" drill where the head coach starts us on the 30-yard line and gives us 8-10 situations to which we must react.

I want to emphasize again that these ratios and formats are examples of the way we have laid out our work week. Your priorities, time lines, and points of emphasis may be entirely different. The important point that needs to be made is the interactive way the total offensive package evolves directly in a proportional manner from game plan to practice structure to actual game calls.

Initially the Vikings' offense practice numbers may seem substantially low to you. Keep in mind that we have only 53 players with which to work each week. As a result, we do not have the numbers that some college and high schools programs may have to provide entire scout teams to be sent off with their respective counterparts to practice for two full hours.

When I was growing up, the mentality and numbers involved with teams enabled football coaches to take large blocks of time and divide their team into separate offensive and defensive practices, each of which utilized the services of a complete scout team. With the reduction in the number of scholarships, and the time limitations imposed on many collegiate programs today, the numbers available to college coaches have considerably diminished. As a result, more and more college teams are adapting their practice formats to those used in the NFL (see page 83).

Scripting

As was pointed out earlier, whatever the parameters you set, it is important to recognize that there is a finite limit to the amount of time you can effectively practice.

The diagram on page 81 illustrates an example of the Script Board that sits next to the Game Plan Board in our offensive meeting room. It shows the total scripted snaps by each situation. By laying out the scripts on this board, we can, at a glance, check the total number of times we are running a given play, from what formations and against what defenses. The script board, like the Game Plan Board, gives each coach a reference point during the week as to what is being scripted, and when. This enables coaches to look at the entire week in one glance and use it for drawing their cards, or for preparing their meetings based on what and where the different parts of the offense are being installed.

Because of the limitations of the number of live snaps that can actually get done during the course of a week, we often prioritize what we think needs to be done vs a live defense and what can be run in a group or individual period. For example, if there is a route progression that we have run a great deal and the players are fairly proficient at, I may not script that route in one of our live periods. In this situation, I conclude that we are familiar enough with the route progression that I can brush it up in an individual or group period and save the live snaps for something new or something that may need the extra work.

Training camp preparation

We use the same method of practice ratios in our training camp preparation as we do during the season. Our training camp basically involves an initial week of preparation culminating in a scrimmage and mock game. The next week then usually involves a scrimmage with another team with the week ending with our first preseason game.

SCRIPT BOARD [PADDED]

WALK THRU
1.
2.
3.
4.
5.
6.
7.
8.
9.
10.
11.
12.
13.
14.

7 ON 7
1.
2.
3.
4.
5.
6.
7.
8.
9.
10.
11.
12.

BASE

TEAM
1.
2.
3.
4.
5.
6.
7.
8.
9.
10.
11.
12.
13.
14.
15.
16.
17.
18.
19.
20.

INSIDE
1.
2.
3.
4.
5.
6.
7.

NICKEL SIT

WALK THRU
1.
2.
3.
4.
5.

TEAM/7 ON 7
1.
2.
3.
4.
5.
6.
7.
8.
9.
10.
11.
12.
13.
14.
15.
16.
17.
18.
19.
20.

NICKEL SIT

WALK THRU
1.
2.
3.
4.
5.
6.
7.
8.
9.
10.

TEAM/7 ON 7
1.
2.
3.
4.
5.
6.
7.
8.
9.
10.
11.
12.
13.
14.
15.

SHORT YARDS
1.
2.
3.
4.
5.
6.

GOAL LINE

WALK THRU
1.
2.
3.
4.

TEAM
1.
2.
3.
4.
5.
6.
7.
8.

BACKED UP (WALK THRU)
1.
2.
3.

The chart on page 83 illustrates how we allot practice time to offensive situations during our training camp. Because most college and high school teams have a similar two-week training camp period, the Vikings' numbers could easily be adjusted to reflect the totals you want to accomplish.

Coaching Assignments

How you utilize your staff when preparing and installing your game plan can be a major asset. It has been well documented that small interactive groups are a much better way to communicate and teach. Furthermore, the time and scope involved with establishing and implementing a game plan makes it very difficult for one individual to effectively do everything. I recognize that you probably don't have as many coaches to work with as we have in the NFL, but delegating responsibilities can be a very effective way of analyzing and formulating the best possible game plan.

An example of the way we divide up our responsibilities is illustrated in the chart on page 84. As you can see, many tasks are divided between two people. Accordingly, if your numbers dictate, you could consolidate several of these functions.

Summary

The key elements in establishing your installation are:

1) *Consolidate* each situation and determine the *size of each package.*
2) Be very aware of *how much overage* you have in each area. The ratio of what you need vs. what can be practiced is vital.
3) Structure your *game plan discussions* and layout so that everyone is on the *same page* as to what is being done.
4) Don't be afraid to *delegate responsibilities* for different aspects of the game plan.
5) Make sure at week's end you have *practiced what you had intended* to practice and have covered all that you have needed to.
6) Make sure each *coach* knows what he is *responsible* for during the game.

VIKINGS' TRAINING CAMP PRACTICE ALLOTMENT — 1995

DAY	PRAC	TYPE	BASE TEAM	BASE SKEL	2ND LONG TEAM	2ND LONG SKEL	3RD LONG TEAM	3RD LONG SKEL	3RD MED TEAM	3RD MED SKEL	SHORT YARDAGE TEAM	SHORT YARDAGE SKEL	GOAL LINE TEAM	GOAL LINE SKEL	RED ZONE TEAM	RED ZONE SKEL	2 PT	BU
MON	1	SHELL	15	14	11	6	10	5	5	4								
MON	2	SHELL		6	5				4	6								
TUES	3	PADS	9	10	5	4	5											
TUES	4	SPECIAL TEAMS PRACTICE																
WED	5	PADS	4	10		4		4		2			5		10	8		
WED	6	SHORTS		4					6	4			6		8	12	2	5
THUR	7	PADS									4							
THUR	8	SPECIAL TEAMS PRACTICE																
FRI	9	SHORTS		10		4	4	4		2	4				4		2	
FRI	10	PADS SPECIAL TEAMS PRACTICE																
SAT	11	SHORTS SPECIAL TEAMS PRACTICE																
MON	12	SHORTS	4	10	4				4	5								
MON	13	PADS	9	8	5				4	8								
TUES	14	SHELL	6	10		4			5	5					10	10		
TUES	15	PADS		10											15	15		
	TOTALS		**47**	**139**	**30**	**52**	**19**	**32**	**28**	**64**	**8**	**8**	**11**	**11**	**47**	**92**	**4**	**5**
WED	16	PADS	6	8					4		4		5		6			
WED	17	SPECIAL TEAMS PRACTICE																
THUR	18	PADS	15	5	4	4			4	5								
THUR	19	SHORTS	6	6			4	4	4	4	3		4		4	3	2	
FRI	20	PADS		5					4		3		4					
FRI	21	SHORTS SPECIAL TEAMS PRACTICE																
SAT	22	SHELL	4	5					2	3					4		2	
SAT	23	SHORTS		4						4								
	TOTALS		**31**	**64**	**4**	**8**	**4**	**8**	**18**	**34**	**10**	**10**	**13**	**13**	**14**	**17**	**4**	**0**

OFFENSIVE COACHES ASSIGNMENT CHART (1996)

Situations	Brian	Ray	Chip	Carl	Mike	Keith
Positions	Off-Coordinator	Quarterbacks	Wide Receivers	Running Backs	TE/OL	OL
Game Analysis	All situations	Nickel Pass, Red Zone Pass, Blitz	Nickel Pass, Red Zone Pass, Nickel catalog	Gen. Run, Sy-GI, Red Zone Run, 4 minute Run	Computer Reports: Self Scout, Opponent Analysis	Gen. Run, Sy-GI, Red Zone Run, 4 minute Run
Scout Report	Game Plan Outline, Route Sheets		Personnel, Cover sheet	Fronts, Run sheets, Pro. sheets	Tendencies	Stunts, Blitz
Week	Scripts	Pass Play Coverages, Team Cards, Blitz Period [Blitz Tape]	Pass Play Coverages, Scout Teams Cov.	Compile Cards, Group Run Cards	Walk Thru Cards, Spec. Cat Cards, Scouts Fronts [Front/Sy/G(Tape)]	Team Cards, 9-7 Cards, Blitz Cards [Sy-GI-2Pt Tape]
Game	Play calling	Secondary	Substition	Call Chart	Front	P.O.A
Half-Time	Coordinate 2nd Half focus and calls Address Off.	Compile Pass Recom. Meet with QB	Meet with WR	Meet with RB	Situation Chart- Compile Run Recom. Meet with TE	Meet with OL

CHAPTER 8

Game Day

Two of the most important aspects of finishing a game plan are how it is laid out for game day calls and how members of the coaching staff approach their assignments on game day.

How a coach lays out his game plan for game day calls is a very subjective matter. It is usually developed after years of trial and error and having things laid out in just a certain way to meet a particular objective. Often the layout is less a function of organization than it is personal preference.

Keep in mind that the game day layout of the offense has to function for the rest of the coaching staff as well. So far, several points have been made in this book about the best game plans being ones that are interactive with both coaches and players. As a result, it follows that the actual layout of a game plan must also serve the purposes of all those involved.

The point has also been made that even though a coach may work very hard to organize the game to flow in a certain manner, things sometimes go awry. Accordingly, the game plan must be laid out so that you can access the plan that was practiced during the week and utilize the plays and formations you prepared, even if it is not quite in the sequence or ratio you had hoped. For this reason, our game plans are laid out in three sections:

   1) sequenced and situation calls
   2) play or special situation
   3) formation and personnel

Even if the game goes according to plan, you may need to make occasional sequential adjustments within the game plan to take advantage of certain plays that seem to be working well or formations and personnel groups that seem to give the defense problems.

If the game is not going along in the sequence you had hoped for, you must be able to access what you have practiced during the week. This is an area where your manner of laying out the game plan is vitally important. If you do not have it laid out in an organized and efficient way, you may end up discarding your plan (and all the work you put into it during the week) and simply wing it.

An example of a type of game day sheet that the Vikings use is presented on page 76. On the far left of this sheet are the situational calls that have been scripted during the week. These are listed in the order I want to call them and are presented to the team in the two meetings on the day before the game.

The center section of the game day sheet is little more than a listing of plays by type: run, pass, play action, screens, etc. It also lists the plays in special categories that are not a part of your normal play-calling sequence on the left.

On the right side of the game plan sheet are the same plays listed by personnel and formations. This sheet is given to the players earlier in the week. This step allows them to prepare with a little more focus on what plays are being run by which personnel, so that those players who may make their major contribution to the game through special plays or formations can focus on the plays in those groupings.

Coaching Assignments
This area can be one of the more difficult parts of implementing a game plan. It can be hard for some coaches to avoid getting caught up in the action and become spectators who watch the game.

It is important that each coach be given a specific assignment and that he maintain his focus on his particular job. We have all been in situations where a player thinks something happened a certain way, when in fact it did not. If you chastise a player for being wrong because you thought you saw it differently, when in fact it was the

Game Day Sheet

Openers	1st/2nd Down	Base Runs	Base Pass	Cov 2	Per/Formation
					(R) Far/Dot
				Blitz	(T) Sprd/Slot
		Draws	Quicks		(T) Twins
	3rd and Long	Nickel Run	Play Action	Best Player	(3) Dbl
Short Yardage	3rd Med	Screen	Action Pass		(3) Train
	+10 / End Zone	Specials			
	3rd Down	2 Minute			
Red Zone +20	Goal Line	4 Minute	Backed Up		
+15	Pressure / 2 Pts	Last 3 Plays	2 Point Chart		(3) Bunch/Vice

85

way the player saw it, not only have you not helped him adjust during the game, but that player may lose a little confidence in your abilities. For this reason, we give each coach a specific part of the play to watch and be accountable for. On the Vikings staff, we assign observation responsibilities as follows:

Receivers Coach:
Watches secondary for coverages, rotations, and match ups.

Running Backs Coach:
Watches backfield action for exchange and drop of quarterback.

Tight Ends Coach:
Watches and charts total front.

Offensive Line Coach:
Watches point of attack

In this way, we can cover a play from all angles. As a result, if a player is confused or makes a mistake, we can have a legitimate answer for him as to what happened and what should have happened.

CHAPTER 9

The Soap Box

I call this chapter "The Soap Box" because it involves some personal perspectives on the direction our profession is going and some coaching aids available to you that I steadfastly advocate.

One of the points that I feel very strongly about is that we have reached the threshold of a veritable explosion of computer technologies that are available, affordable and functional. No one can reasonably deny that every aspect of our lives is being affected by computers. Equally undeniable is the fact that there is no aspect of professional interaction that can be done more quickly, more efficiently, with more organization and more professionally, than with the use of the computer.

Too often people have resisted the technological wave of advancement, thinking that a computer is nothing more than a number-crunching, dehumanizing, complicated mechanism—a device intended for either only the most sophisticated "hackers" or for the games of children. Nothing could be further from the truth.

The very term "computer" is a misnomer. "Communicator" would be a more applicable name to describe what the computer can potentially do for you in our profession. Generally speaking, three areas exist where a coach can genuinely affect the performance of his players and where most advancements in philosophies and principles take place:

- Physical training methods
- Fundamental knowledge (techniques and strategies)
- Teaching methods

In the area of physical training, the body of knowledge has consistently grown over the years with regard to how diet and exercise can enhance a player's performance. Fortunately, much of this information can easily be passed on to your athletes as it becomes available.

Over the years, the body of fundamental knowledge concerning the game has also gone through regular transformations with regard to what are the best techniques and strategies available. In fact, the game has not changed in this regard for quite some time. What changes do take place tend to not be innovative so much as they are cyclical. By this, I mean that styles and tactics go in and out of vogue based on who has won the last Super Bowl. An example of what I am referring to is the famous counter trey play utilized by Joe Gibbs in the Super Bowl days of the Washington Redskins.

The counter trey is a fundamentally sound play that almost all teams have used in one form or another since the mid-80s. As is usually the case, defenses have seen it enough now that they can play the counter very effectively. As a result, the success of this series has diminished somewhat. As the play begins to fade from playbooks to the point that no one really runs it, defenses will next move on to addressing whatever series has taken its place. What the time frame is I can not say for certain, but eventually someone will "re-invent" the counter trey, and because teams have not seen it for awhile, it will again be very successful. Most fundamentals and strategies follow this type of cycle.

That leaves us with the actual teaching methods we use as being the one true area where the most innovations are taking place. It is my opinion that it is this area where you can gain the best "edge" all coaches are constantly looking for to enhance their chances of winning.

I mentioned earlier that I thought one of the keys to Bill Walsh's "West Coast Offense" was less in the actual X's and O's than it was in the innovative approaches he took in installing and implementing those fundamentals. Coach Walsh's offense is a beautifully conceived structure that has had unparalleled success. But those who simply copy the plays used in the system are not able to duplicate its success if they do not take into account the teaching progression that accompanies it.

This point brings me back to my original "soap box". Computers/communicators provide us with an exciting new means with which to coach/teach our players. When I joined the Vikings in 1992, there was not a single PC used by any member of the coaching staff. Today virtually every coach has one.

Even an old-style diehard coach like Bill Parcells in his book, *Finding a Way to Win*, says, "If the competition has laptop computers and you're still using yellow legal pads, it won't matter how long and hard you work, they're going to pass you by."

At this point, I'd like to present a couple of ways we use the PC in our preparation that may prompt some workable ideas for you and your program. First, most people have some form of game analysis program that they use to collate and summarize their opponents' tendencies. In some cases, this is interfaced with your video set up to generate forms of cut-up tapes either for analysis or for teaching purposes.

Short of this you can utilize just a regular spread sheet from any basic program such as Lotus or Excel. By keeping your game analysis or self scout material in this manner, you can very easily and quickly look at any specific aspect of your opponent's defense or your own offense to help you make a play-calling decision during the course of your preparation.

GM	#	DN	DIST	POS	PER	SHFT	FORMATIO	VAR	MOT	PLAY	DISCRIPTION	C/I	#	GAIN	DP	DEF	COV	SNT	BLZ
PIT	1	1	10	-24	R		DOT		HUMP	LIZ	DALLAS	C	87	4	R	UN	1		
PIT	2	1	5	-29	T	SHAFT	TRIPS		ZAP	70	WAGGLE	C	80	8	R	UN	3S		
PIT	3	1	10	-37	R		DOT		HUMP	50	ISO		26	3	R	UN	1		
PIT	4	2	7	-40	T		TRIPS		ZM	BLUE	ORLANDO	I	86	0			1D		D
PIT	5	3	7	-40	3		DBL			LO	479 R FLAT	I	82	0	D	OV	5H		
PIT	6	1	10	-6	T		SPRD	SLOT		50	GUT		26	7	R	UN	3		
PIT	7	2	3	-13	T		TRIPS		WIZ	RIP	DETROIT	C	80	1	R	UN	1		
PIT	8	1	10	-23	T		SPRD		ZM	50	GUT		26	10	R	UN	1		
PIT	9	1	10	-35	H		SOZ			70	CHIP		26	2	R	OV	88		
PIT	10	2	8	-37	3		DBL			RIP	DODGE DBL	C	80	9	R	34	2	X	ZD
PIT	11	1	10	-46	H		SOZ			RED	DETROIT	C	86	12	R	34	4S		
PIT	12	1	10	42	T		TWIN			70	CHIP		26	1	R	34	1		
PIT	13	2	9	41	T		TWIN			FL	O99	I	86	0	R	UN	88		

For example, if you are interested in running a certain route in 3rd and 4-6 and you wanted to check when the last time you ran that progression or how this week's opponent defended this formation in this situation, you could easily find that specific information by sorting the proper categories on your spread sheet.

Often there are specific questions you may have that a larger, more encompassing game analysis report may not sufficiently cover. The time and effort to go back and look at all the film for that specific example may discourage you from finding out the information you need. A spread sheet can make that process much quicker and more efficient.

Another way we use the PC is to draw all of our plays (runs, passes, protections, defenses) and organize catalogues with these schematics for future use. For years, coaches have spent countless hours diagramming plays and formations. In many cases, they are the same plays drawn up the same way. By cataloging our schematics, we can make whatever subtle changes we need for this week's opponent and lay it out for the players to have quickly and with a great deal more detail:

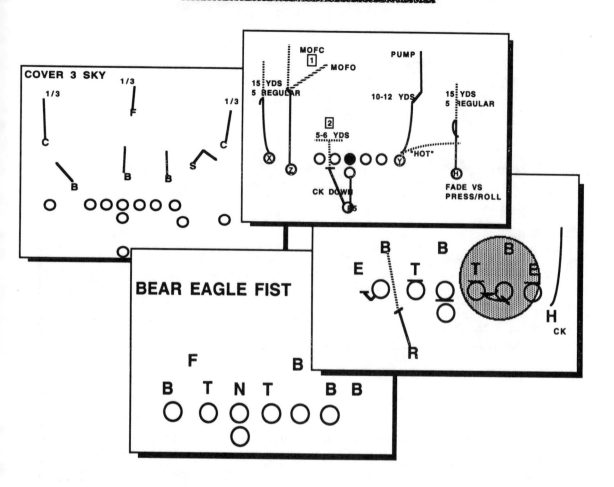

For example, the schematics shown above were done with basic draw programs like Super Paint, Intellidraw, or Visio. Most word processing programs like PageMaker, Word Perfect, and Microsoft Word have this type of basic drawing capability.

All of our scripting is done on a spread sheet that allows us to sort by play and by defense to check our teaching progression and make sure we have covered each play against the proper defensive looks. The spread-sheets on the following page illustrate the comprehensive data that can be provided to coaches:

OPPONENT:			CINCINNATI	DATE:	WED NOV 8	

WALK THRU

NO.	SIT.	HS	P	FORMATION	PLAY	DISCRIPT	DEF
1	BASE	R	R	FAR LT	SCAT LT	816 Y SEAM RM	43 UNDER - 2
2	BASE	L	R	NR RT WIZ	20	OB	EVEN - 4 SKY
3	BASE	L	R	FAR RT	RED	ORLANDO	43 OVER - 3
4	BASE	R	R	NR RT ZEKE	60	CHIP	UNDER - 2
5	BASE	L	R	FAR RT SP	40	ISO	UNDER - 2
6	BASE	R	E	TRN RT HIP	90	WAGGLE	UN NIC - 3S
7	BASE	R	ZE	DBL LT L. SP	RIP	DALLAS	42 NIC - 88
8	BASE	L	R	FAR RT	50	SLIDE 'A'	UNDER - 2
9	BASE	R	3	DBL LT	SCAT LT	H ANGLE DRAG	43 OV NIC - 2
10	BASE	L	3	DBL LT	70	TREY	42 - 88
11	3RD 4	L	3	DBL LT	HI	GIANT	ZN DOG OV NIC - 3
12	3RD 4	R	ZE	TRN LT F. WZ	SCAT LT	816 Y SEAM	UNDER NIC - 8
13	3RD 4	L	E	SPLIT RT	JET RT	DBL DODGE	42 NIC - 3
14	3RD 4	R	4	ROCKET RT F. LP	SPRT LT		
15	3RD 4	M	4	ROCKET RT	60		
16	3RD 4	M	4	ROCKET RT	20		

GROUP RUN

NO.	SIT.	HS	P	FORMATION	PLAY
1	GROUP RUN		R	FAR RT	50
2	GROUP RUN		R	FAR LT	40
3	GROUP RUN		R	NR LT WIZ	50
4	GROUP RUN		R	FAR RT	40
5	GROUP RUN		R	FAR RT	60
6	GROUP RUN		R	NR LT WIZ	70
7	GROUP RUN		R	FAR LT SP	70
8	GROUP RUN		R	FAR LT SP	70
9	GROUP RUN		R	NR RT	60
10	GROUP RUN		3	DBL RT	14
11	GROUP RUN		3	DBL LT	15
12	GROUP RUN		3	DBL LT	20

SPECIAL CAT

NO.	SIT.	HS	P	FORMATION	PLAY
1	BASE	L	R	ZOOM FAR RT	40
2	BASE	R	R	NEAR LT WIZ	40
3	BASE	L	ZE	BUNCH RT	90
4	BASE	R	R	FAR LT SP	70
5	BASE	R	ZE	TRN LT	OPT
6	BASE	R	3	DBL RT	30
7	BASE	R	ZE	BUNCH RT	OPT RT
8	BASE	R	R	NEAR LT	50

OPPONENT:			CINCINNATI	DATE:		

NO.	SIT.	HS	P	FORMATION	PLAY	DISCRIPT	DEF
16	3RD 4	M	4	ROCKET RT	20	BRUSH 'A'	41 - 88
8	GROUP RUN		R	FAR LT SP	70	CHIP	43W
7	GROUP RUN		R	FAR LT SP	70	CHIP	EV
4	BASE		R	FAR LT SP	70	CHIP	EVEN - 2
6	GROUP RUN		R	FAR LT SPEAR	70	CHIP	UNDER - 3 SKY
5	RZ +15	L	H	FAR LT WG	70	CHIP	OV 88
4	RZ +20	R	H	FAR RT WG	60	CHIP	56 WIDE 3
5	GROUP RUN		R	NEAR RT ZEKE	60	CHIP	43 - 2
9	GROUP RUN		R	NR RT	60	CHIP	EV
4	BASE		R	NR RT ZEKE	60	CHIP	UNDER - 2
1	3RD 1	M	J	DOT LT	70	CHIP SOLID	43 SMACK 3
1	3RD 1	M	J	DOT LT	70	CHIP SOLID	56 WIDE 3
5	3RD 1	M	J	DOT LT	70	CHIP SOLID	EAGLE 2
13	GL	M	J	DOT LT F. ZM	70	CHIP SOLID	62 -0
10	GL	M	J	DOT LT F. ZM	70	CHIP SOLID	62 -0
8	GL	M	J	DOT RT F. ZM	60	CHIP SOLID	62 -0
4	BASE		R	FAR LT	30	CUTBACK	UNDER - 3 SKY
8	RZ +20	R	H	FAR RT WG	20	CUTBACK	56 WIDE 3
6	RZ +10	R	H	FAR RT WG	20	CUTBACK	EAGLE 2
2	BASE		R	NR RT WIZ	20	CUTBACK	EVEN - 4 SKY
4	GROUP RUN		R	FAR RT	40	GUT	56
2	BK UP		R	FAR RT	40	GUT	EVEN - 4 SKY
4	BASE		R	NR LT WIZ	50	GUT	EVEN - 2
3	GROUP RUN		R	NR LT WIZ	50	GUT	UN
1	BASE		R	ZOOM FAR RT	40	GUT	43 WIDE-3 SKY TO 2
2	BASE		ZE	ZM TRAIN RT	60	H BEHIND	42 - 2
1	BASE		R	NEAR RT	40	ISO	EVEN - 2
2	GROUP RUN		R	FAR LT SP	50	ISO	OVER - 2
5	BASE		R	FAR RT SP	40	ISO	UNDER - 2
1	GROUP RUN		R	NR RT	40	ISO	UNDER - 2
8	BASE		R	NEAR LT	50	ISO	UNDER - 2
15	GL	M	J	DOT RT F. ZM	20	LEAD	62 -0
11	GL	M	J	DOT RT F. ZM	20	LEAD	62 -0
12	GL	M	J	DOT RT F. ZM	40	LEAD O	62 -0
10	GL	M	J	FOT RT F. ZM	40	LEAD O	62 -0
8	GL	M	J	DOT RT F. ZM	40	LEAD O	62 -0
3	BASE		3	DBL LT FK SP	14	O	42 - 88
11	GROUP RUN		3	DBL RT	14	O	OV NIC - 2
10	GROUP RUN		3	DBL RT	14	O	56
11	GROUP RUN		3	DBL LT	15	O' √ PASS	43 UN

We have also found that by sorting all of our plays by type, formation, and personnel, it gives our players an excellent resource to establish the game plan by whichever way they preferred to learn it. Some players have found the personnel and formation breakdown the best way to learn, while others (like the quarterbacks) preferred internalizing the plays when they were grouped by type. The following diagrams illustrate the two primary methods of sorting plays:

PLAYS BY TYPE

P	FORMATION	PLAY	DISCRIPT	P	FORMATION	PLAY	DISCRIPT	P	FORMATION	PLAY	DISCRIPT
4	ROCKET	20	BRUSH	ZE	BUNCH L. WIZ	SPRINT 19		3	TRAIN	SPEED	JUKE
R	FAR	20	CB	3	DBL	SPRINT 19		3	DBL	SPRINT	JUKE
R	NEAR WIZ	20	CB	R	NEAR ZAP SHAFT	SPRINT 19		4	ROCKET F. LP	SPRINT	JUKE
R	FAR SP	60	CHIP	ZE	DBL L. SP	R/L	DALLAS				
H	WING FAR	60	CHIP	R	FAR SP	R/L	DALLAS	ZE	BUNCH	90	WAGGLE
R	NEAR	60	CHIP	3	SPREAD SLOT SP	R/L	DALLAS	ZE	TRAIN HIP	90	WAGGLE
J	DOT -F. ZM	60	CHIP SOLID	4	TRAIN	R/L	DALLAS	E	SPLIT	90	WAGGLE SP
H	WING FAR	20	CUTBACK	ZE	DBL SP	R/L	DENVER				
E	CHANGE	20	DRAW	4	ROCKET SP	R/L	DENVER	3	BUNCH	JET	SCREEN
R	FAR	40	GUT √	R	FAR SP	QK OPT	DETROIT	E	SPLIT	JET	SCREEN
R	NEAR WIZ	40	GUT √	R	FAR (ZM)	R/B	ORLANDO				
ZE	TRAIN ZM	60	H BEHIND	R	FAR SP	R/B	ORLANDO	ZE	TRAIN F. WZ	SCRAM	7
J	DOT F. ZM	20	LEAD	H	WING	KICK √		ZE	TRAIN	OPT	495
J	DOT F. ZM	40	LEAD O					ZE	TRAIN	OPT	599
3	DBL	14	O	E	SPLIT	JET	DBL DODGE	ZE	TRAIN	OPT	724
R	FAR	60	OUTSIDE	4	ROCKET	SCAT	DBL DODGE	3	TRAIN	OPT	748
R	NEAR WIZ	60	OUTSIDE	R	NEAR ZAP SHAFT	SCAT	FORD	ZE	TRIPS ZEKE	F/L	788
3	DBL	20	PAINT 'A'	3	DBL	H/L	GIANT	3	TRAIN	OPT	989
3	TRAIN	20	PAINT 'A'	3	TRAIN	OPT	GIANT	E	CHANGE	BASE	383 D. T.O
E	CHANGE	40	SLIDE 'A'	3	DBL	SCRAM	44/55	ZE	GANG SP	SCRAM	4 PIVOT M
R	FAR	40	SLIDE 'A'					3	DBL	H/L	585 D. CB
R	NEAR WIZ	40	SLIDE 'A'	3	DBL F. SP	SCAT	H ANGLE DRAG	E	CHANGE	BASE	599 R FLAT
H	WING JUG	40	SLIDE √	R	FAR (ZM)	SCAT	H ANGLE DRAG	R	FAR SP	SCRAM	7 M
3	DBL	20	TREY 'A'	4	ROCKET	SCAT	H ANGLE DRAG	4	ROCKET	SCAT	989 D. CROSS
3	TRAIN	20	TREY 'A'	E	CHANGE	SCAT	R ANGLE	ZE	DBL SP EX	QK SPRINT	DBL PIVOT
3	DBL	60	TREY 'A'	R	CHANGE	SCAT	R ANGLE	E	CHANGE	BASE	DIVIDE R FLAT
4	ROCKET	20	VEER					ZE	GANG SP	F/L	O88
4	ROCKET	60	VEER	ZE	BUNCH L. WZ	F/L	DIG	ZE	DBL HIP	FK 80	SWEEP PASS
3	DBL EX	QB	WEDGE 'A'	4	TRAIN	SCAT	DIG Y SEAM X 8	ZE	BUNCH WIZ	SCRAM	TD M
								ZE	BUNCH OV	OPT	WACO

PLAYS BY PER/FORMATION

P	FORMATION	PLAY	DISCRIPT	P	FORMATION	PLAY	DISCRIPT	P	FORMATION	PLAY	DISCRIPT
3	BUNCH	JET	SCREEN	ZE	BUNCH	90	WAGGLE	R	CHANGE	SCAT	R ANGLE
3	DBL	14	O	ZE	BUNCH L. WIZ	SPRINT 19		R	FAR	20	CB
3	DBL	20	PAINT 'A'	ZE	BUNCH L. WZ	F/L	DIG	R	FAR	40	GUT √
3	DBL	20	TREY 'A'	ZE	BUNCH OV	OPT	WACO	R	FAR	60	OUTSIDE
3	DBL	60	TREY 'A'	ZE	BUNCH WIZ	SCRAM	TD M	R	FAR (RM)	SCAT	816 Y SEAM
3	DBL	SPRINT 19		ZE	DBL HIP	FK 80	SWEEP PASS	R	FAR (ZM)	R/B	ORLANDO
3	DBL	H/L	GIANT	ZE	DBL L. SP	R/L	DALLAS	R	FAR (ZM)	SCAT	H ANGLE DAG
3	DBL	SCRAM	44/55	ZE	DBL SP	R/L	DENVER	R	FAR SP	60	CHIP
3	DBL	SPRINT	JUKE	ZE	DBL SP EX	QK SPRT	DBL PIVOT	R	FAR SP	R/L	DALLAS
3	DBL	H/L	585 D. CB	ZE	GANG	H/L	ZIPPER	R	FAR SP	QK OPT	DETROIT
3	DBL EX	QB	WEDGE 'A'	ZE	GANG SP	SCRAM	4 PIVOT M	R	FAR SP	R/B	ORLANDO
3	DBL F. SP	SCAT	H ANGLE DRAG	ZE	GANG SP	F/L	O88	R	FAR SP	SCRAM	7 M
3	SPREAD SLOT SP	R/L	DALLAS	ZE	TRAIN	OPT	495	R	NEAR	60	CHIP
3	TRAIN	20	PAINT 'A'	ZE	TRAIN	OPT	599	R	NEAR WIZ	20	CB
3	TRAIN	20	TREY 'A'	ZE	TRAIN	OPT	724	R	NEAR WIZ	40	GUT √
3	TRAIN	OPT	GIANT	ZE	TRAIN F. WIZ	SCAT	816 Y SEAM	R	NEAR WIZ	60	OUTSIDE
3	TRAIN	SPEED	JUKE	ZE	TRAIN F. WZ	SCRAM	7	R	NEAR WIZ	40	SLIDE 'A'
3	TRAIN	OPT	748	ZE	TRAIN HIP	90	WAGGLE	R	NEAR ZAP SHFT	SPRINT 19	
3	TRAIN	OPT	989	ZE	TRAIN ZM	60	H BEHIND	R	NEAR ZAP SHFT	SCAT	FORD
				ZE	TRIPS ZEKE	F/L	788				

P	FORMATION	PLAY	DISCRIPT	P	FORMATION	PLAY	DISCRIPT	P	FORMATION	PLAY	DISCRIPT
4	ROCKET	20	BRUSH	E	CHANGE	20	DRAW	H	WING FAR	60	CHIP
4	ROCKET	20	VEER	E	CHANGE	40	SLIDE 'A'	H	WING FAR	20	CUTBACK
4	ROCKET	60	VEER	E	CHANGE	SCAT	R ANGLE	H	WING JUG	40	SLIDE √
4	ROCKET	SCAT	DBL DODGE	E	CHANGE	BASE	599 R FLAT	H	WING	KICK	√
4	ROCKET	SCAT	H ANGLE DRAG	E	CHANGE	BASE	DIVIDE R FLAT				
4	ROCKET	SCAT	989 D. CROSS	E	CHANGE (SWAP)	SCAT	816 Y SEAM	J	DOT -F. ZM	60	CHIP SLD
4	ROCKET F. LP	SPRINT	JUKE	E	SPLIT	JET	D. DODGE	J	DOT F. ZM	20	LEAD
4	ROCKET SP	R/L	DENVER	E	SPLIT	90	WAGGLE SP	J	DOT F. ZM	40	LEAD O
4	TRAIN	R/L	DALLAS	E	SPLIT	JET	SCREEN	J	DOT F. ZM	PP 60	Z FLAT
4	TRAIN	SCAT	DIG Y SEAM X 8	3	CHANGE	BASE	383 D. T.O				

Another technological advance that exists today that has the potential to be a very useful tool for coaches is CD-ROM technology. This technology allows you to take the concept of sorting your plays or your game analysis on a spread sheet and enhances that capability to being able to sort and view the actual video of those plays in the same manner and with the same speed. Right now the only limitation is making CD-ROM technology cost effective enough to make it affordable on the mass market.

In the future, I believe that books of this nature will be accompanied by a CD-ROM that will allow you to access further information on any particular topic in this material, or call up video examples of what is being discussed.

With the time limitations in the off-season that are now placed on college athletes regarding being with the coaching staff, you can easily see the potential teaching properties of a player being able to come by the football office to pick up a disk that he can take home and view on his own. Such a disk may contain a certain series of plays that you want to cover with the athlete, accompanied by printed material, video support, and even videotape of you explaining the series.

If any of this seems far fetched, simply take a stroll over to the computer lab that virtually every school in the nation has on its campus and look at the way these very teaching tools are already being used. If ever you were looking for that little "edge" that might give you the extra dimension you need to make your team just that much better, believe me this is it.

CHAPTER 10

Summary Points

Hopefully you have been able to gain some insight into the way we structure the systematic development of our offensive game plans with the Minnesota Vikings.

The following 10 key points summarize what has been discussed :

1)   You must clearly *identify what your responsibilities* are as the offensive coordinator (play caller) of your team.

2)   You must constantly *analyze the methods* you are using to implement your game plan and determine the capabilities of the group of players you are dealing with each year.

3)   Determining the *size and scope of the offense* you wish to run in any given year or game is the single most important aspect of developing your game plan.

4)   In creating your game plan, you should keep the four key measures of *turnovers, explosive plays, 1st down efficiency ,and Red Zone efficiency* in mind.

5)   You should establish an *opening sequence* that can be identified, practiced, and implemented by the entire coaching staff and offensive team.

6)   You should identify the *parameters* of every situational offensive segment and identify the *measurable success* of each segment and how you are going to achieve those levels of success.

7)   You should have a *plan for every conceivable contingency* your team will face, no matter how unusual the circumstances may seem.

8)   You should be as *detailed and specific* as your time and materials allow.

9)   You should make sure you are *using all the tools* available to you.

10)   You should recognize that the most important factor in your game plan is the *human element,* and that the way you interact with your coaches and players affects any and all preparations you make.

The main points covered in each chapter were as follows:

An important factor in your game plan should be the "human element."

Introduction

The key elements in developing your offensive package are:

1) *Define your job* as "offensive coordinator" and the approach you will take.
2) Recognize that above all else you are a teacher and *determine the capabilities* of your students/players and the best *methods of teaching/coaching* them.
3) Keep in mind that preparing any game plan involves four main elements:

   - Determining size and scope of the offense
   - Outline situational offensive needs
   - Implementation of game plan
   - Game day needs

4) Remember that the number one element in approaching each of the aforementioned four areas is to be as *detailed and specific* as your time and materials allow.
5) Keep the *four "key" measurable categories* in mind when formulating your game plan:

   - Turnovers
   - Explosive Plays
   - 1st Down Efficiency
   - Red Zone Efficiency

How Much Offense?

The key elements in determining how much offense you should carry are:

1) Think on *three levels* when determining how much offense you can run: *yearly, weekly, and on game day.*
2) Take the time to *determine exactly* the *size and scope* of each critical situation you will face.
3) Work hard to *keep your overage* of plays to *25-30%.*
4) Take the time to *review each week* the amount and nature of offense you ran and see if your planning stayed within the *expected norms* you set for yourself.

Base Offense

The key elements in establishing your base offense are:

1) *Determine size and scope* of the package you need.
2) Determine if a recognizable *difference* exists between *1st down and 2nd and long.*
3) *Establish* an *opening sequence* and be specific with regard to what you want to run and then *stick by it.*
4) Keep your *opening sequences interactive* with regard to *personnel and formations.*
5) Keep your *opening priorities* in mind:

> • *Get a 1st down*
> • *Keep yourself in a convertible 3rd down distance*
> • *Create an "explosive"*

3rd Down

The key elements in establishing your 3rd down package are:

1) Determine *the size and scope* of your package.
2) Recognize the *success ratio* you can expect in each phase:

> • *3rd and long   (20-25%)*
> • *3rd and medium (45-50%)*
> • *3rd and short   (75-85%)*

3) Leave your *options* open for your quarterback and be certain he *understands what those options are.*
4) Have a *plan* to handle the *blitz.*
5) Match your *plays* by *personnel and formation.*
6) *Determine* your plan for 3rd and *short* during the week and *stay with your plan.*

Pre-Red Zone and Red Zone

The key elements in establishing your Red Zone package are:

1) Determine the *size and scope* of your package.
2) Determine the *abilities of your kicking game* and once inside field goal range, *never* put yourself in position to be *taken out of that range.*
3) Remember that this is an area where you must have the *most detailed* part of your game plan and should eliminate as many "surprises" as you can.
4) Coordinate your +10, Goal Line, and two-point plan to be *interactive.* Be prepared to carry one aspect of the plan into the other.

Special Category
The key elements in establishing your special category package are:

1) Determine the *size and scope* of each package, even if it is unlikely it will come up.
2) Coach your players to *understand the unique properties* of each of these situations.
3) Stress the *importance* of each situation and reinforce the fact that it may come down to one of these situations to *win a game*.
4) Make sure that the players know your *intentions* in each of these situations and that they do not *misinterpret* your actions in these situations as *panic*.

Installation and Game Plan
The key elements in establishing your installation are:

1) *Consolidate* each situation and determine the *size of each package*.
2) Be very aware of *how much overage* you have in each area. The ratio of what you need vs. what can be practiced is vital.
3) Structure your *game plan discussions* and layout so that everyone is on the *same page* as to what is being done.
4) Don't be afraid to *delegate responsibilities* for different aspects of the game plan.
5) Make sure at week's end you have *practiced what you had intended* to practice and have covered all that you have needed to.
6) Make sure each *coach* knows what he is *responsible* for during the game.

The very fact that you are reading this book indicates you are one of those types of individuals who is constantly looking to improve your craft and be the best coach/ teacher you can be.

I commend you for your efforts and hope that this material might be of some small help in your endeavor to prepare a winning football team.

About the Author

Brian Billick

Offensive Coordinator
Minnesota Vikings

After setting a team record and finishing third in the NFL in offensive output with 5,848 yards in 1994, the Vikings' offense, under the tutelage of offensive coordinator Brian Billick, surpassed that record and ranked fourth in the League with 5,938 yards last year. The 1994 and 1995 totals were the two best back-to-back finishes by the Minnesota Vikings offense in NFL history.

In addition, Minnesota set a team season record in 1995 for points scored with 412, which also ranked fourth in the NFL. The Vikings also tied team records for consecutive 30-point games with four and 30-point games in a season with six in 1995.

In 1994, Billick guided a unit with eight new starters to match the franchise's highest finish (3rd in 1974) ever in the NFL in total offense. Minnesota also placed second in the NFL in pass offense (4,324), the team's highest finish since 1981 when it also was second. In addition, those passing yards were the second most in a season in team history to the club-record 4,333 yards in 1981.

The passing game has not been the only beneficiary of Billick's tutelage. Last year, four different backs rushed for 75 or more yards in a game. Among those was Robert Smith, who was fifth in the NFL in rushing and on pace to a team season rushing record when he suffered an ankle injury in the seventh game. Since Billick became offensive coordinator three games into the 1993 season, three different backs have each had three 100-yard rushing games.

After taking over the Minnesota offense in 1993, Billick oversaw a unit that made dramatic improvements as the season progressed. The Vikings went from 264.8 yards per game over the first six weeks of the year to a 323.3-yard average over the season's final 10 games. During the season-ending three-game winning streak that propelled Minnesota into the playoffs, the offense averaged 351.7 yards and 21.6 points per game and did not yield a single sack.

Prior to joining Minnesota, Billick tutored wide receivers and tight ends at Stanford, where he developed wide receivers Ed McCaffrey and Chris Walsh, and tight ends Ryan Wetnight and Jim Price. McCaffrey earned All-America honors in 1990 and has been with the New York Giants, San Francisco, and Denver. In 1991, Walsh caught 66 passes, the second most by a wide receiver in school history. In his NFL career, Walsh has played for Buffalo and Minnesota.

During Billick's stint as offensive coordinator at Utah State from 1986-88, quarterback Brent Snyder set a school season record for passing yards with 2,887 in 1987. He then surpassed that mark with 3,218 yards a year later.

From 1981-85, Billick served as recruiting coordinator and coached receivers, tight ends and quarterbacks at San Diego State. During his stint with the Aztecs, Billick helped tutor quarterback Todd Santos, who set the all-time NCAA passing yardage mark; wide receiver Webster Slaughter, a Pro Bowl selection during his NFL career; and tight end Rob Awalt, the NFL Rookie of the Year with the Cardinals in 1987.

Billick began his coaching career as an assistant at the University of Redlands in 1977. He then spent a season as a graduate assistant, working with tight ends and the offensive line, at Brigham Young University. Billick was the Assistant Public Relations Director for the San Francisco 49ers in 1979-80.

Born in Fairborne, Ohio, Billick earned three letters in football and basketball, and was a Helms Scholar-Athlete as a senior at Redlands (CA) High School. Brian and his wife, Kim, have two daughters, Aubree and Keegan.

ADDITIONAL FOOTBALL
RESOURCES FROM

COACHES CHOICE

■ *COACHING LINEBACKERS*
by Jerry Sandusky and Cedric Byrant
1995 ▪Paper▪ 136 pp
ISBN 1-5716-059-9 ▪ $15.00

■ *COACHING OFFENSIVE BACKS*
by Steve Axman
1996 ▪Paper▪ 230 pp
ISBN 1-57167-088-2 ▪ $19.00

■ *THE BUNCH ATTACK*
by Andrew Coverdale and Dan Robinson
1996 ▪Paper▪ 256 pp
ISBN 1-57167-044-0 ▪ $19.00

■ *101 DEFENSIVE FOOTBALL DRILLS*
(3 VOLUMES)
by Bill Arnsparger and James A. Peterson
1996 ▪Paper▪ 128 pp▪ $15.00 each
Vol #1, ISBN 1-57167-084-x
Vol #2, ISBN 1-57167-085-8
Vol #3, ISBN 1-57167-086-6

TO PLACE YOUR ORDER:
U.S. customers call
TOLL FREE (800)327-5557,
or write
COACHES CHOICE Books, P.O. Box 647, Champaign, IL 61824-0647,
or FAX: (217) 359-5975